ETIQUETTE and PROTOCOL

A Guide for Campus Events

BY APRIL L. HARRIS

CASE. Books

Council for Advancement and Support of Education (CASE) is
the professional organization for advancement professionals at all levels
who work in alumni relations, communications, and development.

CASE offers high-quality training, information resources, and
a wide variety of books and materials for advancement professionals.

For more information on CASE or a copy of our books catalog,
visit our Website, *www.case.org,* or call (202) 328-5900.

Book design: Fletcher Design
Editors: Ellen Ryan and Laura Henning
Cover photo: Bruce Carroll/Tony Stone Images

CASE. Books

Council for Advancement and Support of Education
1307 New York Avenue, NW
Suite 1000
Washington, DC 20005-4701

TABLE OF CONTENTS

Foreword

WHEN I WAS IN GRADUATE SCHOOL AT
Emory University studying medieval British history, my
advisor and major professor was George Peddy Cuttino, a
leading medievalist. George, as he preferred to be called, was a native of Newman,
Georgia, and had been a Rhodes Scholar. His D. Phil was from Oxford, where he
was a member of Oriel College. Having drunk fully from that well of tradition,
George was also marshal of Emory University and chair of its academic ceremonies
committee.

On the subject of academic ceremonies, he was without an equal and from
him I acquired my interest in that field. I remember well the care that he lavished
on every part of Emory's ceremonial life; his pleasure at watching the Emory mace
borne in the convocations by the Student Body president was one of pride. As well,
I remember the care he took working with the vergers who assisted processions
almost as "outriders". Emory was participating in a 900 year-old tradition.

Think of the University: your university or mine. Heirs of a 900-year-old
legacy, the University is younger than few other institutions—the church being the
prime one. And the University grew, as April Harris reminds us, under the
sheltering gown of the church.

I suspect it was my training as a medieval historian that caused Victor
Hurst, Clemson University's Vice President for Academic Affairs, to ask if I would
plan the inauguration of a new Clemson president. I looked to literature for a guide
and found little. Gunn's *A Guide to Academic Protocol*, although charmingly out-of-
date, was one. Sheard's *Academic Heraldry* was another. Venable and Clifford's
Academic Dress of the University of Oxford was a third. Still another was the large file
at CASE's office in Washington, DC. Having read them, I consulted George. He
was a great help. One of his suggestions was to watch with analytical mind the
ceremonies of the Anglican Church, which proved most helpful.

Over the years, my wife and I had spent a great amount of time in the
United Kingdom and from time-to-time had attended services in the churches of
England and Scotland. There we had gained in a visual sense the reinforcement of
George's advice.

During my time of planning that Clemson inauguration, I attended, as Clemson's representative, a number of inaugurations of presidents of other colleges. Some, such as the College of Charleston's, were tasteful and helpful. Others were dreadful. Along the way, I have been privileged to witness, as Clemson's representative, centennials, inaugurations, investitures, installations, convocations, and what have you.

Through it all, I have been struck by a number of things. First, despite occasional faculty or administrative grumpiness, proper etiquette matters a great deal to most people. It matters to a mother weeping with joy as her daughter, the first in the family to graduate, marches behind a bagpiper at commencement at a small church-related college; and it matters to a proud father and children watching as a son, newly commissioned as a second lieutenant and displaying his bars on the simple black bachelor's gown over his uniform, walks up the ramp to receive that precious diploma at a major state university.

I wish April Harris's book had been available when I tackled my first academic ceremony because it sets forth the best practices in our ancient tradition. Harris's explanations are clear and sensible; moreover they are up to date. The tradition she sets before us and the courtesy she asks of us are important. That tradition should be maintained not only for our sake but also, more importantly, for the sake of our students and their proud, happy, and jubilant families.

Jerome V. Reel, Jr.

Jerome V. Reel, Jr.
Senior Vice Provost and Dean of Undergraduate Studies
Clemson University

Preface

THIRTY YEARS AGO, MARY KEMPER GUNN wrote *A Guide to Academic Protocol* on the basis of her experiences at Columbia University. She was one of the first to recognize that "on the administrative staff of every university, college, and similar institution there is (or should be) someone who is responsible for putting the institution's best foot forward on public occasions." Her handy little book has long been out of print, but much of her advice has stood the test of time. (For example, "your most valuable asset is the appearance of calmness no matter what beyond your control may go wrong at the last moment.")

The greatest change since Ms. Gunn wrote her guide is in the status of women. In 1969, women were still primarily supporting characters to their faculty husbands. Her book is sprinkled with such advice to women as this, "A good rule is that any time you would wear white gloves you should also wear a hat. This includes commencement, a daytime convocation, a formal luncheon, an afternoon reception." Or imagine today saying, "Some time during the week before commencement, ten or twelve attractive secretaries must be borrowed from various offices on campus to help with the robing of the dais party, and a time set aside to teach them the details of robing."

When I started working in public relations on campus in the 1970s, it seemed every institution had its own resource person like Mary Kemper Gunn. For me, it was a woman on the president's staff who could supply us neophytes with the answers to any question about etiquette, good taste, or procedure. Today most of these advisers are gone, but the need to maintain their standards and pass their knowledge along to the next generation of campus events planners is stronger than ever. It is in this spirit that I have undertaken this project.

Like our language, etiquette is fluid and ever changing. It is easy to find conflicting advice from experts on what would seem to be fairly straightforward questions. The degree of formality taken for granted on one campus might seem out of place on another. I have worked on a campus where all faculty and staff were addressed exclusively as "Dr.," "Ms.," or "Mr."—not only by students but by colleagues. I have also worked for a university where everyone, including the president, was on a first-name basis.

As special events planners, we are the keepers of campus traditions and responsible for presenting our institutions graciously and properly every time we welcome guests. This book is not the all-encompassing final answer for every question and situational nuance that you will face. (There are many comprehensive etiquette books on the market today to steer you through specific, unusual situations that you may face only once in your career.) Instead, it is an easy-to-use compendium of advice for situations that planners confront daily.

Much as editors create style rules to regulate the capitalization and punctuation used in our publications, special events planners need to develop a consistent style or standard for campus etiquette. Repeated rituals become traditions. Whether your campus is inclined toward morning coats and tails on commencement or family picnics under the trees following the ceremony, hospitality must be delivered uniformly, gracefully, and consistently. Observing institutional manners forges the next link in the chain of academic tradition that extends back to medieval times. In a contemporary interpretation, such manners are an integral part of institutional image.

My special thanks to Dr. Jerome V. Reel, Jr., senior vice provost and dean of undergraduate studies at Clemson University, for sharing his expertise on academic traditions; to Ms. Dorothea Johnson, director, The Protocol School of Washington, for providing me expert training; and to my editor, Ms. Victoria Welling, for her sharp blue pencil.

As Mary Kemper Gunn said in her introduction, "Let the new people, wherever they are, proceed with confidence."

April L. Harris
February 1999

CHAPTER 1

Invitations

*A*S RECENTLY AS THE 1920s, INVITATIONS were handwritten and delivered to guests' homes by a servant. Guests knew their polite obligation to reply within a few days and did so. (In the Victorian era, the expected response time was 24 hours.) Once an invitation was accepted, especially for dinner, it was unthinkable to fail to appear. In 1922, Emily Post wrote, "Nothing but serious illness or death or an utterly unavoidable accident can excuse the breaking of a dinner engagement."

Today invitations are often computer generated and sometimes sent by bulk mail, and getting people to reply at all is a real accomplishment. Often, those who do accept change their minds without the courtesy of canceling their reservations. Regardless, invitations can be among the most important and enjoyable components of events.

The invitation creates the first impression of your event and is often the basis people use to decide whether or not to attend. On campus, invitations can range from fliers photocopied on colored paper, to business letters, to complicated sets of formal invitations for a rare occasion like the inauguration of a new president. All invitations, whether to a black-tie affair or to a small luncheon at your president's home, should meet the highest standards of taste, quality, and correctness.

This is not to say that all invitations must look formal and seem stuffy, although there are plenty of occasions for which only the most traditional invitation will do. Fortunately, the casual, multifaceted nature of entertaining on campus permits an acceptable degree of creativity, provided that standards of quality remain in place. This means planning every invitation and accompanying inserts with care, checking and double-checking that all names are spelled correctly, and assuring that there are no typos and that dates, times, and phone numbers are accurate.

The way your invitation looks—"sophisticated," "important," "fun," or "boring"—often does more to convey the tone and character of your event than do the words. Special event invitations should match other printed materials associated with the event. One events planner refers to printed materials as the "footprint" of the event, noting that such items are all that is left behind to tell your story. Varying the paper, or stock, you choose according to texture, weight, color, and finish can give each invitation a unique personality. A distinctive paper, an eye-catching design, or both can ensure that your invitation gets opened.

• • •

The Precedence of Extending Invitations

Most colleges and universities have several special weekends each year that are packed with activities and events. The highlight of the fall calendar may be a reunion or parents' weekend that includes meetings of the university and alumni boards of trustees, several meals, private functions at the president's home, a football game with pregame brunches and tailgating, entertaining in the president's stadium box, an alumni black-tie gala, and a Sunday-morning breakfast. On these occasions, alumni, donors, trustees, parents and others can be barraged with a confusing batch of invitations to a variety of functions all occurring at approximately the same time. On most campuses, because guest lists are not well coordinated between offices and because a person can easily fall into several categories (an alumnus may be a donor, a trustee, and a parent), his or her name may appear on several guest lists. The result is a stack of invitations for various functions issued by different offices. Not only does this make it seem as if no one on campus knows what anyone else is doing, it puts guests in awkward positions.

What if a guest receives an invitation from the alumni association for pregame brunch and a few days later receives an invitation to the president's pregame brunch? Normally, the president's invitation would take priority over the alumni association's, but if the guest received the alumni association's first and replied affirmatively, he or she is obligated to decline the president's invitation rather than break the first commitment. Few people, however, would want to risk offending the president by turning down his or her invitation.

The failure of events planners to coordinate plans and guest lists creates problems across the board. First, it puts guests in unacceptable situations by forcing them to pick and choose or try to squeeze too many events into too little time. Often people will not say yes or no to any invitation, attempting instead to appease everyone by "floating" in and out of functions. Not only does this make for a harried weekend for the guests, it creates havoc with everything from name badges to tickets, food guarantees, and seating arrangements. Some people resolve the question of which function to attend by simply "no showing" at certain functions. Again, planners are left with empty seats at meals, unused name badges, and tickets that must be paid for even though no one used them.

In fairness, many guests make the logical assumption that functions are coordinated and that one group must know what the other has planned. People assume that if they receive an invitation from the president, it supersedes others and that organizers know that their names have been moved "up" to the president's list, thus releasing them from earlier obligations.

Here is the correct precedence for issuing invitations:

- The types and times of events and their guest lists should be coordinated among offices while planning is in the early stages, especially for busy weekends and large celebrations like anniversaries or inaugurations. Determine the most appropriate hosts and functions for each person or group of people. The president is the ranking campus administrator. His or her guest list should be prepared first, and those invitations should be mailed before any others. Invited guests of the president should not be invited to other functions that occur at the same time.
- On occasions hosted by university trustees, that group takes precedence. Invitations from the trustees are often issued jointly with the president. In that case, the wording would be

The Board of Trustees and President
of Major University
request the pleasure of your company

- Once the president's invitations have been issued, invitations for other functions can be sent. A good rule of thumb is to wait one week.
- There is often competition for important guests among the colleges and the offices of alumni, development, public relations, and athletics. One way to resolve such conflicts is to assign guest lists to important functions by looking at the events calendar as a whole. If, for example, the college of arts and sciences is having an alumni day on a football weekend, either exclude key constituents from entertaining done that day on behalf of the president or make the entire group the president's special guests. Duplicate events can sometimes be avoided by simply including development officers or other college representatives on the guest list of functions hosted by the president or deans.
- On some weekends, guest lists simply must overlap. One solution is to time functions so that people can attend several. If the president is inviting alumni to brunch and then to her box for a football game, but there is no postgame function, it is acceptable for another group to invite her guests to a postgame affair. It would not, however, be acceptable for another department to invite the same people to the football game. A word of warning: Be very careful about inviting only some people who have attended an activity to a subsequent function, as hurt feelings can result. You can help avoid this situation by putting a reasonable amount of time between your gathering and the one that preceded it and by making certain the host and purpose of your function are clear. This works best when the original group is composed of a mixture of constituents. Consider the following scenario: The president's football guests have included legislators, prominent parents, and alumni, including several distinguished arts and sciences graduates—and the college of arts and sciences is hosting an evening reception for its graduates. It is acceptable for the college to invite

its distinguished alumni who were hosted that afternoon without inviting the president's entire guest list. If, however the president had hosted a group made up exclusively of arts and sciences alumni, it would not be acceptable to invite only a few of them to a college reception.

• • •

Coordinating Invitations from Several Offices

Commencements, inaugurations, anniversaries, convocations, and other university-wide events often include the coordination of complex invitations, reception cards, VIP passes, parking credentials, and the like. For example, platform participants at commencement receive a different set of invitations and credentials than guests who will watch the ceremonies.

Send all of the invitations pertaining to the event in one envelope. Doing so gives the guest the opportunity to have an overview of the day as opposed to having invitations arrive over the course of several days or weeks. When several offices are arranging components of a special occasion, all invitations should be of the same quality. It is not necessary that they match graphically, but they must match in terms of correctness and taste.

Once the guest replies affirmatively, send the appropriate credentials and passes in one neatly organized packet.

• • •

Some General Guidelines for Creating Invitations

The form and feeling of a printed invitation must be consistent with the type of event you have planned. Casual events permit a level of creativity, but when a formal affair is planned, only a formal invitation will do.

Choose a traditional ink color. Black is the most correct choice, and if you are producing very formal invitations, black is required. For less formal occasions, alternative ink colors that are acceptable and easy to read include dark blue, deep green, brown, and dark burgundy. Avoid metallics and light or bright colors.

Type styles selected by your graphic designer should be easy to read. Helvetica, Times New Roman, and Garamond are tried and true. The preferred and most correct font for formal invitations is script.

In the past, invitations were hand-engraved. The resulting sharp lines and raised texture were reminiscent of the hand calligraphy once used in monasteries to copy official documents and announcements. Because an engraver actually hand-cuts each letter into a copper plate, the process has become cost-prohibitive for most people. Real engraving can be identified by looking at the back of the page, where you'll find indentations caused by the pressure of the printing press when it forces the paper into the grooves of the printing plate.

Today, the two most commonly used methods for printing invitations are offset printing and thermography. Offset lettering has no raised texture but offers the advantage of producing sharp, clear lettering at a very affordable cost. Offset is sometimes referred to as "flat printing." Thermography does create a raised texture. It is most commonly seen on wedding invitations and business cards. In this process, the lettering starts out the same as offset lettering, but a final step is added. While the ink is still wet, it is dusted with a powdered resin. The sheets then pass through a heated tunnel, and the powder melts, forming a clear, raised surface over the lettering. The disadvantage of thermography is that it often isn't as sharp as offset printing.

• • •

The Components of an Invitation

An invitation should answer who, what, when, where, how, why, and "so what." After reading your invitation, a potential guest should have enough information on which to base a decision. Unfortunately, many invitations omit the purpose of the gathering, the name of the person extending the invitation, or both.

The purpose of the event should be clearly stated in small type at the top left-hand corner of the invitation or in the middle of the body of the invitation. There are many acceptable phrases for doing so:

- In honor of [insert the person's name]
- To commemorate the anniversary of or the successful completion of or the ribbon cutting for. . .
- To meet [insert the person's name]
- To kick off the [insert the name of your] capital campaign
- To announce a large grant or gift
- To congratulate [insert a person's name] on her award, recognition, promotion, or retirement
- To celebrate the occasion of attracting 100 National Merit Scholars, the opening of a new building, winning an NCAA National Championship in Ice Hockey, or the like

Invitations come from people, not entities. It is correct to say, "The Board of Trustees of Major State University requests the pleasure of your company. . ." because the board is made up of people. It is incorrect to say, "Major State University requests the pleasure of your company."

Letitia Baldrige teaches what she calls the 10 elements of an invitation. Learning and remembering them will help ensure that you always convey all important information. Here is her formula:

Line 1: The organization's symbol. This could be the college or university seal or logo embossed or printed at the top or bottom of the invitation. It should be small enough to be tasteful and unobtrusive. It is smart to keep a supply of invitations on hand that have been printed with the university seal. Doing so saves money and time and helps ensure quality and consistency.

Line 2: The names of the hosts. On formal invitations extended for official university entertaining, use the host's full name (Sumter August Moore, junior). The person's title goes on the second line. Omit honorifics such as Dr., Mr., Mrs., and Ms. unless the person holds an official rank, such as mayor, judge, state senator or representative; is a member of Congress or the President's cabinet; or is a diplomat or a military officer.

On an informal invitation, it is acceptable to use the host's nickname (Sumter Moore). When there are several hosts, the most senior person's name is listed first:

Sumter A. Moore, Jr.

President

and

Charles P. Jones

Director of Athletics

request the pleasure of your company

If you want to list the hosts on the same line, the most senior person's name appears on the left-hand side:

Sumter A. Moore, Jr., President   Charles P. Jones, Director of Athletics

request the pleasure of your company

When the invitation is from a committee and the people are of approximately equal business or social rank, list the members alphabetically at the top of the invitation. Omit honorifics except for persons with official rank. List the names in two or three columns if necessary.

If the invitation is from the university president and his spouse, say

Dr. and Mrs. Sumter A. Moore, Jr.

When both are Ph.D.s, or M.D.s, say,

Dr. Sumter A. Moore, Jr. and Dr. Marian Applebee Moore

When she uses her maiden name:

Dr. Sumter A. Moore, Jr. and Dr. Marian Applebee

Line 3: This line extends the invitation. Its phrasing is dictated by tradition. "Requests the pleasure of your company at" is the most formal. "Cordially invites you to" or "invites you to join us" are less formal.

Line 4: Tell the kind of event you are having. This is usually a one- or two-word statement. It could be as simple as "dinner," "a reception," "lunch," or "cocktails."

Line 5: Tell the purpose of the event: "in honor of the 1998 President's Scholars" or "to welcome the university's new provost."

Line 6. The date. On a formal invitation, write it out: "Friday, the twelfth of February." Less formal invitations can use the more common version, "Friday, February 12."

Line 7: State the hour. On formal invitations, times are written out: "at nine o'clock," "at half after six o'clock."

Line 8: Tell the place, including street address. For campus buildings, state the room within the building, building name, and street address (Alumni Memorial Gallery, 13 Old Main Hall, 2100 Campus Drive). If you are using a hotel or other off-campus property, state the full name, street, and city (University Inn, 333 Mountain View Drive, Logan).

Line 9: This is the bottom right-hand corner of the invitation, and it is reserved for special instructions. Messages that can be placed here include "black tie," "dancing," "invitation not transferable," "this invitation admits one only," "valet parking," "map enclosed," "rain date," "please present this invitation at the door," "tickets will be held at the door," "jacket and tie required for men," and so forth.

Line 10: The R.S.V.P. information. If you are issuing a traditional formal invitation without an R.S.V.P. card, print the address and telephone number of the person handling replies. People should notify you of their intentions within a week, preferably by a handwritten note.

If you are supplying R.S.V.P. cards, use the statement "R.S.V.P. card enclosed."

For more informal invitations or when time won't permit waiting for replies to be returned by mail, simply use R.S.V.P. and a phone number.

Don't use the phrase "regrets only"; people tend to disregard it.

Resist the temptation to put a cutoff date under R.S.V.P. Doing so is not correct, and there is little evidence to show it works.

• • •

Issuing Formal Invitations

Formal invitations follow a time-honored format that varies only in the smallest details. Formal invitations use a traditional script typeface, although Shaded Roman or Shaded Antique Roman are considered acceptable. Print the invitations in black ink using thermography or engraving on high-quality white or ecru stock. The most traditional format is a plain card measuring 4 1/2 inches wide by 5 3/4 inches tall or 4 3/4 inches wide by 7 1/4 inches tall. A double-fold invitation printed on the first page, like those used for weddings, is also correct.

It is attractive and correct to print the institution's official seal or logo at the top of the page. If your budget permits, produce the seal in blind embossing. The image is not inked.

Wording the Message

- Word the invitation in the third person.
- Use full names written out: Sumter August Moore, junior. Note that the word "junior" is written in lowercase when spelled out. When abbreviated, use a capital J (Jr.).
- Use titles: President and Mrs. Sumter August Moore, junior.
- The phrase "request the pleasure of your company" is used most often. If you are inviting high-ranking or very distinguished people, the phrase "request the honor of your company" is most appropriate.

- The date is spelled out. Only the day and month are capitalized: "Saturday, the fifth of September" or " Saturday, September fifth."
- The hour is spelled out. Times are written as "six o'clock," "at half past six o'clock" or from "six until eight o'clock" You may also say "six-thirty o'clock," or "from six-thirty to eight-thirty o'clock." Noon is indicated as "twelve noon" or "twelve o'clock."
- Addresses should be written out unless the number cannot be written in a few words: "Thirty-one Hillside Drive" but "1310 Hillside Drive."
- Avoid using any numerals other than phone numbers.
- Abbreviations are not used with the exception of Dr., Mrs., Mr., and R.S.V.P. or R.s.v.p.

Dress

A formal invitation traditionally meant black tie, and everyone knew it. Today, it is necessary to write "black tie" on the lower right-hand corner of the invitation.

R.S.V.P.

The most formal invitations do not include an R.S.V.P. card. Instead, the address for replies is printed below the R.S.V.P. line. Formal invitations do not include a telephone number for R.S.V.Ps. This is because, traditionally, good manners dictated that the recipient would immediately pen a written response. Many etiquette purists still hold to this standard and find printed R.S.V.P. cards highly offensive. However, special events planners know an R.S.V.P. card is essential if we are to have any hope of determining an accurate guest count. Thankfully, most people now consider an R.S.V.P. card acceptable and have come to expect one.

Complete the invitation by including a matching printed R.S.V.P. card and a self-addressed envelope. It is not necessary to supply postage on the reply envelope. When you supply an R.S.V.P. card, do not also print the reply address on the invitation.

If maps, ticket-order cards, or other special instructions are needed, they too should be printed to match.

Is it R.S.V.P. or R.s.v.p.? R.S.V.P. is an abbreviation for the French phrase "repondez s'il vous plait" (please respond). It can be written in upper case (R.S.V.P.) or R.s.v.p. Choose the form you prefer, and stick with it so that usage is consistent on all of your invitations.

Envelopes

Envelopes should be of good quality and match the invitation. Print your return address on the flap. Be sure there is adequate adhesive on the flap to render the use of tape or additional glue unnecessary.

Addressing the Invitations

The computer has been a blessing and a curse to the fine art of addressing invitations. On one hand, computers are an enormous help in keeping track of people and their addresses and how often and to which functions they have been invited. On the other hand, computers have depersonalized the invitation process. The ability to spit out hundreds of addresses at the press of a button means that time-consuming, handwritten addresses are being replaced by fast but ugly labels. What's worse, computers and the limited space on database files have made it easy to drop the use of people's titles.

The beauty, prestige, and personal nature of a formal invitation demand a handwritten address that includes titles. The use of gummed labels, even the clear ones currently in vogue, is incorrect and in poor taste. Never use them. Plan to have formal invitations hand addressed by a calligrapher or someone who has beautiful and legible handwriting. Some mailing houses offer this service or keep lists of free-lance calligraphers. You pay by the address. To ensure adequate time for hand-addressing, order the envelopes ahead of the printed invitation's delivery date so that addressing can begin immediately. Before beginning, research your mailing lists and telephone people whose titles are missing or are of questionable accuracy.

- Addresses should be written with a black fountain pen or a black roller-ball pen in order to achieve fluid, beautiful lines.
- If hand-addressing is not feasible, the second best alternative is a computer-generated or typewritten address directly on the envelopes using black ink.

Postage Stamps

Send formal invitations by first-class mail. Doing so is a subtle way of reinforcing the extra-special nature of the occasion and also helps increase the chance that your invitation will be opened and read. Select an attractive commemorative postage stamp for this purpose, preferably one that reinforces the event theme or that is consistent with an education theme. Never use a postage meter.

If institutional policy demands that, for budgetary reasons, invitations be bulk mailed, have the bulk indicia neatly printed on the envelope so that the ink matches the rest of the job. Remember to allow extra mailing time to compensate for the slower service given this class of mail.

Stuffing the Envelopes

Insert the invitation into the envelope so that the folded side is at the bottom of the envelope. The invitation's front or printed side should peek out of the V cut into the flap side of the envelope so that when the person opens the envelope and pulls the invitation out, it is face up in reading position. When using a card-style invitation, insert it so that the printed side faces up. The left-hand side of the card goes to the bottom of the envelope so that when it is pulled out, the sentences are in reading position.

Stack the R.S.V.P. card and other inserts on top of the invitation so they cannot be missed. A plastic-coated paper clip or other attractive clip can be used to hold the inserts together.

When to Mail

Generally speaking, the more prestigious the event and the busier the season, the sooner invitations should be mailed. Knowing the customs of your area will greatly help you gauge the best timing, but four to six weeks is standard for a major event or for a breakfast, luncheon, dinner, or evening reception. Three weeks is sufficient for an afternoon tea, a reception, or a cocktail party.

• • •

Types of Invitations

Special Events and Fund-Raising Invitations

Colleges and universities have created a hybrid version of entertaining. We invite guests to events and then ask them to pay for the privilege of attending! Such occasions constitute a large part of campus special events planners' duties and include everything from reunion weekends, concerts, lectures, workshops, and recognition programs to, of course, fund-raising events. Invitations to these functions, especially fund-raising events, display a wide range of imagination and creativity and are as much marketing pieces as they are true invitations.

Work with your graphic designer early on to create an attractive look that can be used for all aspects of the event from invitations to name badges. A well-designed creative invitation package may make the difference in how many people decide to support your event. But although there is room for creativity, planners must supervise the invitation design to be certain it meets standards of taste and quality consistent with the institutional image. One of the biggest challenges is fitting all needed information regarding ticket sales, parking, program times, and schedules into a limited amount of space.

Your first obligation to your guests is to be certain the invitation clearly communicates all pertinent information about who, what, when, where, how, and why the event is being offered.

After this, creativity and colorful graphics are acceptable and fun. A note of caution: Check postal regulations to be certain a proposed design will conform to size and weight limits to avoid paying extra postage on nonstandard mail.

When the event is a fund raiser or if you are selling tickets or taking reservations for a variety of activities by asking guests to select from a menu of choices, the main body of the invitation should stick to communicating the basics of what is happening. This includes time, place, and who's hosting. Event details and necessary check-off blanks are presented on insert cards. Here are some pointers:

- Committee members should be listed in the invitation package because their names lend prestige and credibility to the event. Committee members can be listed on the inside right-hand panel of a double-fold card, on the back of the invitation, or, if the list is short, at the top of the invitation. List the chair first followed by an alphabetical list of committee members. Be consistent about the use of honorifics and the format of names. "Mr. and Mrs. Stanley P. Jones, Mr. and Mrs. Ralph D. Hawthorne, Mr. and Mrs.

Wolfe P. Hammacker" is consistent and correct. Or, more informally, "Stanley and Roberta Jones, Ralph and Betty Hawthorne, Wolfe and Sue Hammacker." Avoid a mishmash such as "Mr. and Mrs. Stanley P. Jones, Ralph and Betty Hawthorne, Mr. Wolfe and Sue Hammacker."

- Ticket prices should be stated on the reply card, not on the invitation.
- The reply card should have spaces to fill in the name, address, and phone number of the person responding and lines to list persons with whom he or she would like to be seated.
- For fund-raising events that offer various ticket levels, use the reply card to detail special perks awarded the purchaser at each level.
- If part of the ticket proceeds represents a charitable contribution, U.S. law demands that you notify donors of the fair market value of the event. The reply card is often used to state the amount of the ticket price that constitutes a tax-deductible contribution, but providing this information does not substitute for sending a receipt. Make sure you understand how these amounts are to be calculated and what donor-notification process is required. Charities can receive hefty fines for failing to comply.
- Provide a line on the reply card for the recipient to make a donation if he or she cannot attend the event.
- Enclose an unstamped return envelope addressed to the person responsible for recording replies. Caution: If you are using bulk mail, this address must match the address for which your bulk-mail permit was issued. In other words, if you are using the university bulk-mail permit, replies cannot be sent to the off-campus address of a committee member.

Save-the-Date Cards

Extremely important university functions that the "right" people simply must attend require notification as far in advance as possible. To accomplish this, "save-the-date" cards are sent six months to a year in advance and can help get your event on busy people's calendars. Save-the-date cards are particularly important for presidential inaugurations, anniversary commemorations, capital campaign kickoff events, and occasions once in the history of an institution, such as major building dedications. If you are counting on participation by government officials, corporate executives, or institutional celebrities, save-the-date notices are essential. Save-the-date cards are also advised for multiple-day meetings, such as board meetings and retreats, or when international guests are included.

Special events planners who sense that an extremely busy social season might affect attendance at an important event sometimes issue save-the-date cards about six weeks ahead of invitations to preempt other groups' invitations and to start building interest in and support for an event.

The format for producing a save-the-date card is simple. Print a postcard-size announcement that states the occasion, date, hosts, and type of event in very brief terms. Center the lines of type on the card as follows:

Please hold the date of
Saturday, September fifth
for the New Century Capital Campaign Kickoff dinner
given by the Board of Trustees
of Major State University
Redrock, Utah
(Invitations to follow)

As an alternative, the final line of the announcement could say "details will follow."

The most difficult part of issuing a save-the-date card is that doing so requires setting the general framework of the event and deciding a preliminary, but fairly accurate, guest list sometimes months in advance. It is especially nice if save-the-date cards match the invitation design, although this is not mandatory. Keep accurate records of those who receive the cards to ensure that they also receive invitations.

Fill-in Invitations

Fill-in or skeleton invitations are preprinted cards that tell the name and title of the person extending the invitation and have a number of blank places for writing in the particulars of the occasion. Cards are usually 6 inches wide by 4 1/2 inches tall on stiff stock, usually ecru in color with matching envelopes. Fill-ins are regarded as semiformal invitations and are excellent for inviting guests to official, yet less formal events like campus luncheons, small receptions, or functions at the president's home that involve 100 or fewer guests. (If you are inviting more than 100 people, have an invitation printed.) Keeping a supply of fill-ins on hand is particularly handy for the president, vice presidents, deans, and other academic officers whose duties frequently require them to entertain or host other functions.

Guests are expected to respond to fill-ins with a phone call or short note.

The format for a fill-in is this:

THE PURPOSE WRITTEN IN

The New Century Capital Campaign
Planning Committee

Sumter A. Moore, Jr.

President, Major University

requests the pleasure of your company

at *lunch*

on *Friday, April 1*

at *Noon*

Alumni Dining Room
University Center, 300 Campus Drive
Logan

R.S.V.P.
000-555-1212

Business Letters as Invitations

Invitations to meetings, small luncheons, or combinations of meetings with social activities (such as an afternoon meeting followed by a cocktail hour) can be extended in a letter on campus letterhead. As always, the invitation should supply all information necessary for the guest to decide whether or not to attend. Don't use R.S.V.P.; instead, state the method for replying in the body of the letter. For example, "Please let my assistant, Julia Smith, know of your intentions."

Electronic Invitations

E-mail and fax are now integral parts of business communications and may be used for extending certain invitations. Notices of meetings, invitations to working luncheons, and the like are appropriate uses of this technology. The problem with both e-mail and fax is that communications aren't always private and can seem impersonal. Most faxes are ugly. Never use fax or e-mail as a substitute for a formal invitation.

Because computer terminals and fax machines are often shared, electronic invitations should include the full name, title, and office name of the recipient. Also, the full name, address, and phone number of the sender are imperative.

Reminder Cards

If invitations have been extended by telephone or in person, it is a good idea to send reminder cards to ensure that guests have all the particulars. Reminder cards should match your fill-in invitations in stock, typeface, and ink color. The typical size is 3 1/2 inches wide by 4 3/4 inches tall. Reminder cards have blanks to be filled in with the function, time, and place. The heading consists of the host's name and title and should be printed. The function's purpose can be written in the upper left-hand corner.

PURPOSE LINE (LONG RANGE PLANNING COMMITTEE)

New Century Campaign Committee

To remind you that
Sumter A. Moore, Jr.
President, Major University
is expecting you
for *lunch*
on *Friday, April 1*
at *noon*
Alumni Dining Room
University Center, 300 Campus Drive
Logan

CHAPTER 2

Forms of Address

Is it Miss, Mrs., or Ms.? Ph.D. or Professor?
The Honorable or Mayor?

ONORIFICS, THE TECHNICAL TERM FOR forms of address, can be confusing. Once taught to all schoolchildren as a form of respect for their elders, the use of proper forms of address is now often neglected. American informality has blurred understanding about when and with whom titles should be used. Formality in the workplace varies among regions of the country and from industry to industry. In some organizations, everyone from the CEO on down is on a first-name basis; in others, colleagues unfailingly address one another as "Ms." or "Mr." In the Southern United States, youngsters are still taught to address women as "ma'am" or to honor the old custom of addressing a married woman who is a family friend as "miss" coupled with her first name ("Miss Jane"). In contrast, in the western part of the United States, surnames seem to be a long-forgotten formality.

The computer also has contributed to the erosion in use of proper forms of address. Many organizations that lack the staff to research and record personal preferences and that face limited space on computer files have dropped honorifics altogether. This is incorrect. While titles may seem unnecessary to many people, for those who have attained them through years of dedication to their careers, titles are important badges of honor. Paying close attention to proper forms of address can set your invitations and correspondence apart and subtly convey your respect for others. Being more formal than expected is never a disadvantage; rather, such courtesy shows respect and is flattering to the recipient.

There are three keys to success in knowing what to call people. First, know the culture of your campus and abide by its rules. Second, know when and how to use correct forms of address when dealing with "outsiders." Finally, when in doubt, always use the most formal form of address.

First Names

It is always most correct to address a person by his or her honorary title ("Mr.," "Ms.," "Mrs.," "Dr."). Never presume the right to address the person by his or her first name. Wait until he or she gives you permission to use it. As a general rule, anyone who is older than you should be addressed by his or her title. Train student workers to know and use this rule. It is very inappropriate for college students to immediately address professors, administrators, office workers, and campus visitors by first name. Always err on the side of formality. This courtesy is imperative when hosting international visitors.

Miss, Mrs., or Ms.

"Ms." is now accepted as proper for women, regardless of their marital status. The adoption of "Ms." was intended to demonstrate that women's professional and individual identities are independent of their marital status. It is correct to address women of all ages by "Ms."; however, many older women prefer the traditional "Mrs." or "Miss." The best course is to find out each woman's preference beforehand and note it in your files. If you are sending invitations to a couple and you know the woman prefers to be addressed as Ms., use Mr. followed by his name and Ms. followed by her name on the same line ("Mr. Henry Smilings and Ms. Virginia Smilings"). Do not link Ms. to the husband's name: "Mr. and Ms. Ralph Jones" is incorrect.

Many women choose to be known as Ms. professionally but use Mrs. in their social lives. In such a case, if you were inviting Sarah Adams to speak at a convention, she would be addressed as "Ms. Adams." If, however, you were inviting Sarah and her husband George, to a social event, they would be addressed as "Mr. and Mrs. George Adams."

Use "Miss" when addressing women under age 18.

Female Donors

Women who make gifts independently of their husbands deserve special attention with regard to form of address. Many computer programs are set up to key off of the male's name and spit out donor acknowledgments in his name. Never presume to issue a joint thank-you or to divide credit for a gift between husband and wife when it has been given by a woman, particularly if the check is drawn on her company account. When in doubt, telephone her for clarification.

Use of the Married Name

When a married woman uses her husband's name, address invitations to both of them using his given name and their surname: "Mr. and Mrs. Ralph Jones." It is incorrect to address a married woman as Mrs. when using her first name ("Mrs. Kathleen Jones"); that indicates she is divorced. When an invitation is addressed to her only, use "Mrs. Ralph Jones" or "Ms. Kathleen Jones." When the husband's name includes the designation "Jr." or "Sr.," use it in addresses, especially if junior and senior live in the same town.

Use of the Maiden Name

To address a married couple when the woman has kept her maiden name, use this form: "Mr. Stanley Blackthorn and Ms. Lucinda Smythe," written on the same line. If you can't fit both names on one line, put hers on the second line preceded by the word "and." Indent it three spaces.

An Unmarried Couple Who Live Together

To address an unmarried couple who live together, write the names in alphabetical order on two lines without indenting the second line: his on the first ("Mr. Hampton Lake") and hers on the second ("Ms. Gretta Long"). Do not link the names by the word "and."

A Woman Who Outranks Her Husband

When the woman outranks her partner by virtue of an elected office or military rank, her name precedes the male's name regardless of the couple's marital status. For example, if she is a mayor, the proper format would be "The Honorable Rebecca Linn and Mr. Robert Linn."

Ph.D.s

You may properly address individuals with Doctor of Philosophy degrees (Ph.D.) by using either the abbreviation Dr. before their names or the initials Ph.D. after, but not both. "Dr. Quantum Physics, Ph.D." is incorrect. Instead use "Quantum Physics, Ph.D." If you are uncertain as to whether a person holds a Ph.D., find out before making a mistake that will embarrass you both. In conversation, Ph.D.s are referred to simply as "doctor."

M.D., D.D.S., D.V.M.

If you are associated with a university that has a medical, dental, or veterinary school, avoid confusion about who is a medical doctor and who is a Ph.D. by adopting a consistent policy for using these abbreviations. Refer to medical doctors with the abbreviation Dr. preceding their names or M.D. following. Indicate Ph.D.s by using that abbreviation following their names. Many medical school faculty are M.D.s and Ph.D.s but choose to use only one title, depending on whether they are practicing medicine and teaching medical students or conducting research. When in doubt of an individual's preference, ask.

Doctors of Dental Surgery use the abbreviation D.D.S. Veterinarians use D.V.M. to indicate Doctor of Veterinary Medicine. In conversation, and on personal and social correspondence, both should be referred to as "doctor."

Dr. and Dr.

When addressing invitations to a husband and wife who are both Ph.D.s or both medical doctors and who share a surname, use either "Drs. Boyer "(eliminating first names) or "Dr. Gene Boyer" and "Dr. Sally Boyer," written on the same line.

Chancellors, Presidents, Deans, and Professors

College and university presidents and chancellors typically hold Ph.D.s (check to be sure). When addressing invitations or correspondence to them, either precede the name with the appropriate title or use Ph.D. following the name, but don't use both. Either "President Annette Jacobs" or "Annette Jacobs, Ph.D" are correct. On some campuses, the president is addressed in conversation by that title. If the president or chancellor does not have a Ph.D. or M.D., address him or her as "Mr." or "Ms."

Deans are typically addressed in conversation as "Dean So and So" or by the title Dr., if applicable. If the dean does not hold a Ph.D. or M.D., "Ms." or "Mr." is appropriate.

At American universities the title "chancellor" means the chief administrative officer. As such, the chancellor would outrank everyone else on campus with the exception of the university board of trustees. In practice, the chancellor is not always the top administrator. The term is sometimes awarded as a ceremonial office to a much-beloved campus administrator in his or her final working years, and, in some places, a president outranks a chancellor. At one Texas college, the chancellor is on campus every day, but his duties are minimal. The president is the true ranking administrative officer and is very much in charge of day-to-day operations.

The status and responsibilities of the chancellor can also vary among state systems. In California, each state university has a chancellor, and the entire system is run by a president who, of course, outranks the individual chancellors—an arrangement that is opposite of that used elsewhere. When working with chancellors, research exactly which type you are dealing with.

Professors

It is important to know the culture of your campus before referring to all faculty as "professor." On some campuses, the title is used informally to indicate anyone who teaches; on others, it is jealously reserved for those who have attained the official faculty rank of professor. When using the title, drop other honorifics and don't use Ph.D. after the name. Simply write "Professor Jane Smith," not "Professor Jane Smith, Ph.D."

With professors and associate professors who hold Ph.Ds, use "Dr." or a "Ph.D." after their names. Professors who don't hold doctorates should be addressed as "professor," if that is the tradition on your campus, or simply as "Mr." or "Ms."

Professional Designations

Many people use initials following their names to indicate professional status or achievements (for example, C.P.A., which stands for certified public accountant). The use of professional titles should be reserved for business. When a person uses such a designation, drop the use of "Ms." or "Mr." before the name on invitations or in correspondence. Use "Ann Armstrong, C.P.A.," not " Ms. Ann Armstrong, C.P.A."

Don't use professional initials in social situations. When addressing a personal letter or an invitation to the individual or to a couple, drop the professional initials and use "Mr.," "Ms.," or "Mrs." The exception to this rule is never substitute "Ms." or "Mr." for "Dr."

Esquire

The term esquire is most commonly used to refer to lawyers, although some court officers are also entitled to use it. Write it following the person's name: "Jo F. Jones, Esquire." When using it, drop "Mr.," "Ms.," or "Dr." It is incorrect to say "Ms. Jo F. Jones, Esquire." Also, do not use "Esquire" in conversation. Instead, address an attorney as "Mr." or "Ms."

Another option for addressing lawyers is to use "Attorney at Law" instead of "Esquire." Write out this phrase on the second line of a lawyer's address. Use the honorific "Mr." or "Ms." preceding the full name, and don't also use "Esquire." (Line 1: Ms. Jo F. Jones; line 2: Attorney at Law; line 3: address.)

The Honorable

American federal, state, and local government officials are referred to by the courtesy title "The Honorable." Write this on the line above the person's full name. It is preferable not to use the abbreviation "The Hon." People who have earned this title may be addressed as such for life; however, they should not use it to refer to themselves. Do not address a person in conversation by this title. Instead, use "Mr.," "Ms.," "Mrs.," or "Dr." It is acceptable to use "The Honorable" in platform introductions.

Military Officers

For those who have never served, military titles can be mysterious and confusing. All officers are addressed by rank. Disregarding their titles is inexcusable.

There are five military services in the United States: Air Force, Army, Coast Guard, Navy, and Marines. Each has its own traditions and protocol. Ranks are not equal from branch to branch of the services. A captain in the Navy holds a much higher rank than a captain in the Air Force. The rank of lieutenant is used in all branches of service but has a greatly different value in each one.

When writing an officer, a full, proper address also includes the branch of service. The abbreviations for the services are as follows: USA (Army), USAF (Air Force), USCG (Coast Guard), USN (Navy), and USMC (Marine Corps). Follow this format for written communication: full rank, full name, service branch (for example, "General George Washington, USA"). If you don't have enough room to get everything on one line, put the full title on line 1, full name on line 2, and branch of service on line 3. When writing a retired officer, use the full rank, full name, service designation, and then "retired" on the line beneath. (line 1: General; line 2: George Washington; line 3: USA; line 4: Retired; line 5: street address). The abbreviation "Ret." is also used, but it is more correct to write out the word retired.

• • •

Frequent Encounters—A Quick Reference

University President or Chancellor

Most university presidents or chancellors hold Ph.D. degrees. If not, address them as "Mr." or "Ms." The titles "president" and "chancellor" are not interchangeable. When in doubt, double-check.

ADDRESSING AN ENVELOPE:
> Dr. Roberta J. Tucker
>> President (or Chancellor)
>> Institution's Full Name
>> Street Address

ON AN INVITATION: Dr. Roberta J. Tucker or President Tucker

PLACE CARD: President Tucker or Dr. Tucker

INTRODUCTION: President Tucker or Dr. Tucker

CONVERSATION: Dr. Tucker or President Tucker

Academic Officers (provost, vice presidents)

Provosts almost always hold Ph.D.s. Most vice presidents do not. Always check.

ADDRESSING AN ENVELOPE:
> Dr. (or Mr. or Ms.) William T. Smith
>> Title
>> Name of Institution
>> Street Address

INVITATION: Dr. (or Mr. or Ms.) Smith

PLACE CARD: Dr. Smith

INTRODUCTION: Dr. Smith, university provost, or Mr. Smith, vice president for development

CONVERSATION: Dr., Mr., or Ms. as appropriate

Deans

American tradition is that deans are usually referred to as "Dean" and their surname instead of as "Dr.," "Mr.," or "Ms." If a dean holds a Ph.D., it is acceptable to address him or her as "Dr." or "Dean." Otherwise, use "Mr." or "Ms." or "Dean."

ADDRESSING AN ENVELOPE:
> Dean Marie M. Hodge
>> Name of College or School (e.g.,College of Business Administration)
>> Name of Institution
>> Street Address

INVITATION: Dean Hodge or Dr. Marie M. Hodge, Dean of the College of Business Administration

PLACE CARD: Dean Hodge or Dr. Hodge
INTRODUCTION: Dean Hodge or Dr. Hodge
CONVERSATION: Dean Hodge or Dr. Hodge

Administrative Staff (athletic director, bursar, development director, PR director, registrar)

Use "Dr.," "Mr.," or "Ms." as appropriate.
ADDRESSING AN ENVELOPE:
 Mr. Jack P. Johnson
  Athletic Director
   Name of Institution
   Street Address
INVITATION: Mr. Johnson
PLACE CARD: Mr. Johnson
INTRODUCTION: Mr. Johnson
CONVERSATION: Mr. Johnson

Professors

Use "Dr.," "Mr.," or "Ms." as appropriate.
ADDRESSING AN ENVELOPE:
 Dr. William T. Parks or Professor William T. Parks
  Name of College or Department
   Name of Institution
   Street Address
INVITATION: Dr. William T. Parks
PLACE CARD: Dr. Parks or Professor Parks
INTRODUCTION: Dr. Parks or Professor Parks
CONVERSATION: Dr. Parks or Professor Parks

Distinguished Professors and Professors of Endowed Chairs

Some professors hold prestigious chairs or have gained a special designation such as university or trustee professor in recognition of career accomplishments. Some professors hold several titles, and an events planner can be faced with line after line of copy trying to fit all of them in a small space. Use the title that is most prestigious and drop the rest. Here is an example for a professor who holds an endowed chair.
ADDRESSING AN ENVELOPE:
 Dr. Jonathan Q. Dewitt
  Flutter-Peabody Chair in Economics
   College of Business Administration
   Name of Institution
   Street Address
INVITATION: Dr. Jonathan Q. Dewitt

PLACE CARD: Dr. Dewitt or Professor Dewitt

INTRODUCTION: Dr. Jonathan Dewitt or Professor Dewitt, the Flutter-
Peabody Chair in Economics

CONVERSATION: Dr. Dewitt or Professor Dewitt

Associate Professors, Assistant Professors, Instructors

Use "Dr.," "Mr.," or "Ms." as appropriate.

ADDRESSING AN ENVELOPE:
 Dr. Ralph H. Frisky
  Associate Professor
   College of Engineering
   Name of Institution
   Street Address

INVITATION: Dr. Ralph H. Frisky

PLACE CARD: Dr. Frisky

INTRODUCTION: Dr. Ralph Frisky, College of Engineering

CONVERSATION: Dr. Frisky

Emeriti and Retired Faculty and Staff

Faculty (and occasionally staff) are sometimes honored at retirement with the designation "emeritus" and continue to use their academic titles. Retired persons who do not hold emeritus status do not continue to use their academic titles.

ADDRESSING AN ENVELOPE:
 Dr. Sandy A. Lane
  Professor Emeritus of English
   Name of Institution
   Street Address

INVITATION: Dr. Sandy A. Lane

PLACE CARD: Dr. Lane

INTRODUCTION: Dr. Sandy Lane, professor emeritus of English

CONVERSATION: Dr. Lane

Student Leaders (Government, Greek Organizations, Clubs)

ADDRESSING AN ENVELOPE:
 Mr. or Ms. Full Name
  Title, Organization Name
   Name of Institution
   Street Address

Government Officials

The President of the United States

ADDRESSING AN ENVELOPE:

    The President

     The White House

      Washington, DC 20500

       Invitation: The President

When issuing a joint invitation to the president and his wife: The President and Mrs. Washington (The first lady is never referred to by her given name.)

PLACE CARD: The President or the President of the United States

INTRODUCTION: The President or the President of the United States

CONVERSATION: Mr. President (Never address the president by his or her first name.)

The First Lady

Never use the first lady's given name or her initials. She is known by surname only while her husband holds office.

ADDRESSING AN ENVELOPE:

    Mrs. Washington

     The White House

      Washington, DC 20500

INVITATION: Mrs. Washington

PLACE CARD: Mrs. Washington

INTRODUCTION: Mrs. Washington

CONVERSATION: Mrs. Washington

Former U.S. Presidents

When a president completes his term of office, he is entitled to use the title as a courtesy, but there are subtle changes in the way it is used. First, he is no longer addressed as "the president." Instead, drop the word "the" and simply say, "President Roosevelt." His wife once again uses his full name (Mrs. Theodore Roosevelt, instead of just Mrs. Roosevelt.) When addressing an invitation to them jointly, the address now includes his full name ("President and Mrs. Theodore Roosevelt" instead of just "President and Mrs. Roosevelt"). In speaking, it is acceptable to address the former president by that title or simply use "Mr." If he is retired from a high-ranking military position, he can also choose to use that title ("General Eisenhower") instead of president.

The Vice President of the United States

ADDRESSING AN ENVELOPE:

    The Vice President

     United States Senate

      Washington, DC 20510

INVITATION: The Vice President
PLACE CARD: The Vice President
INTRODUCTION: The Vice President
CONVERSATION: Mr. Vice President

Note: The spouse of the vice president is addressed as Mrs. His Full Name. When there is a male vice presidential spouse, he would be addressed as Mr. His Surname.

United States Senators

ADDRESSING AN ENVELOPE:
  The Honorable
   Ralph Jones
    United States Senate
     Washington, DC 20510
INVITATION: Senator Jones
PLACE CARD: Senator Jones
INTRODUCTIONS: Senator Jones or the Honorable Ralph Jones, United States Senator from State Name
CONVERSATION: Senator Jones or Senator

United States Representatives

ADDRESSING AN ENVELOPE:
  The Honorable
   Mary Smithfield
    House of Representatives
     Washington, DC 20515
INVITATION: Ms. Smithfield
PLACE CARD: Ms. Smithfield
INTRODUCTION: Ms. Smithfield or the Honorable Mary Smithfield, Representative from State Name

Governor of a State

ADDRESSING AN ENVELOPE:
  The Honorable
   Mary Pat Jordan
    Governor of Ohio
     Street Address
INVITATION: The Governor of Ohio
PLACE CARD: The Governor of Ohio
INTRODUCTION: Governor Jordan or the Honorable Mary Pat Jordan, Governor of the State of Ohio
CONVERSATION: Governor Jordan or Governor

State Senators or Representatives

ADDRESSING AN INVITATION:
   The Honorable
      Bryan Ridge
         Alabama State Senator (or Representative)
         Street Address
INVITATION: Mr. Ridge
PLACE CARD: Mr. Ridge
INTRODUCTION: Mr. Ridge or the Honorable Bryan Ridge, Alabama State
   Senator (or Representative)
CONVERSATION: Mr. Ridge

Mayors

ADDRESSING AN INVITATION:
The Honorable
   Bernice Jane Bright
      Mayor of Portland
      Street Address
INVITATION: The Major of Portland
PLACE CARD: Mayor Bright
INTRODUCTION: Mayor Bright or the Honorable Bernice Bright, Mayor of
   Portland
CONVERSATION: Mayor Bright or Madam Mayor

Judges

ADDRESSING AN INVITATION:
The Honorable
   Betty Dickenson
      Judge, Name of Court
      Street Address
INVITATION: Judge Dickenson
PLACE CARD: Judge Dickenson
INTRODUCTION: Judge Dickenson or the Honorable Judge Betty Dickenson,
   Name of Court
CONVERSATION: Judge Dickenson

Note: the most correct and traditional format for writing addresses on envelopes is to indent each line three spaces to the right.

· · ·

Look It Up

There are many rules with many subtleties for addressing U.S. and foreign government officials, religious leaders, and military officers. In fact, entire books are available on this subject alone. While this brief list is adequate for most everyday occasions on campus, it is inadequate when you are welcoming international visitors. Before you host international visitors, do some research. Etiquette and protocol vary widely from culture to culture, and people from other countries are much more mindful of the proper use of titles than are Americans. Failure to address a foreign visitor properly can cause serious offense. Do your homework by consulting an up-to-date resource for the country from which your guests come. If you live in a large city, call the consulate of the country located there, or telephone the country's embassy in Washington, DC, and ask to speak to the cultural attache. Other excellent sources include Letitia Baldrige's business etiquette books or *Protocol: The Complete Handbook of Diplomatic, Official and Social Usage* by Mary Jane McCaffree and Pauline Innis.

CHAPTER 3

Receiving Guests

$\mathcal{A}$S SPECIAL EVENTS PLANNERS, IT IS OFTEN our duty to make introductions. Failure to make introductions is noticed and causes embarrassment and discomfort for those around us.

In today's gender-neutral etiquette, introductions are based on precedence (who outranks whom). Gender does not affect the order of introductions.

These are the rules for making introductions:

- A younger person is introduced to an older person.
- A peer at your institution is introduced to a peer from another institution.
- A nonofficial person is introduced to an official person (official persons are those who hold elected or government offices).
- A junior administrator, faculty member, or executive is introduced to a senior administrator, faculty member, or executive.
- A colleague is introduced to a guest.
- The name of the highest-ranking, oldest, or most distinguished person is always spoken first: "Mr. Older Person, I'd like to introduce to you Mr. Younger Person." "President from Another University, I'd like to introduce to you President from Our University."
- Always stand for introductions.
- Respond to an introduction by repeating the person's name ("Hello, Mr. Smith."). Don't just say "hi."
- If you use an honorific with one person's name, use an honorific for everyone: "Mr. Smith, I'd like to introduce to you Mr. Jones," not "Mr. Smith, I'd like to introduce to you Phil Jones."
- Don't give yourself an honorific ("Hello, I'm Mary Smith," not "Hello, I'm Ms. Mary Smith."
- If you forget someone's name, admit it and lighten the situation with a little humor.
- If you are misintroduced, correct the error immediately, but do it in a friendly way.

· · ·

Name Badges

Whether it's pinned on, clipped on, stuck on, or hung on, one thing is for certain: The perfect name badge has yet to be invented.

Socially acceptable "cheat sheets," name tags spare us the embarrassment of having to admit we've forgotten someone's name. Bosses demand them (in extra-large type, please, so that the name can be read without glasses), ladies in silk dresses loathe them, and event planners resent the time and effort expended making sure they're correct. Technically, the only time it is appropriate to use name badges is in a business setting like a luncheon, convention, or large meeting. It is not proper to ask guests at a function in a private home or club or at a black tie affair to don name badges—a philosophy most advancement professionals won't adopt anytime soon. Like it or not, name badges are here to stay.

Regardless of what type you choose, badges should be professionally prepared. Never toss a pile of stick-on name tags and a stack of felt tip pens on the table so guests can write their own. If you must supply name badges for dressy affairs, hire a calligrapher to hand-letter them or choose a computer font that resembles calligraphy. Lettering should be readable from about three feet.

Badges should be worn high on the right shoulder for easy viewing during introductions and should contain the person's first and last name and company name if it is pertinent. Include city and state only if guests hail from many places. Omit courtesy titles (Ms., Mrs., Mr.), but use professional titles (Dr., Mayor, Major).

Have extra matching badges at the venue (and the pen or computer that created the originals) to accommodate walk-in guests or to correct errors.

To identify staff, use ribbons attached to their badges with the word "host" or "staff," or print the information on their badges. Speakers should not wear a name badge during their presentations.

Offer a variety of badge styles (clip, pin, cord) to accommodate those who don't want to stick a badge on their clothing. If a person objects to wearing a badge, don't force the issue.

· · ·

Introducing a Receiving Line

When you are hosting 60 or more people, a receiving line is the most gracious (and fair) way to ensure that guests of honor and invited guests have the chance to meet and greet one another properly. It lends an air of significance to your event and helps prevent the honoree from feeling monopolized, overwhelmed, or isolated.

Receiving lines are also excellent tools for facilitating introductions when the campus president is new or is hosting a function for guests he or she may not know.

Here are some guidelines for properly managing a receiving line at an official event:

- Select an appropriate location. The line should form near the event entrance but should not obstruct the doorway or block access to food or drink, or otherwise create a traffic jam.

- Keep it short. For a business function, keep the number of people in the receiving line to a minimum. They should include the guest or guests of honor and the hosts. Regardless of whether the guest of honor or the campus officials are male or female, spouses do not need to be included. The exception is when the honored guest is from out of town or from another country. In this case, the spouse can be included; protocol dictates that the spouse of the host must also stand in line. Beyond this, the number of people who compose the line is up to you. Consider adding a few key people who are associated with the occasion, such as a dean or vice president. But remember that increasing the number adds to the likelihood that the line will bog down.

- If there are multiple hosts and the event is large, it is acceptable to rotate those who stand in the receiving line.

- Make it go smoothly. A protocol officer, special events staffer, or someone else who is good with names and knows the guest list well should serve as the introducer. This person stands at the beginning of the receiving line and greets each guest. The guest either says his or her name or gives the introducer a small card on which it has been clearly written. The introducer then guides the guest to the host—the first person in line—and makes an introduction. The introducer then returns to his or her place to greet the next guest. Simultaneously, the host introduces the people who have just been presented to the guest of honor, who is stationed on the host's right. After a very brief hello, the guests then continue down the line on their own, introducing themselves and shaking hands with each person.

- Keep it moving. Assign staff assistants to help move people along. Duties include encouraging talkative guests to continue through the line to the next person and preventing people from congregating at the end of the line and thus creating a traffic jam. Station a staff member at the end of the line to direct people into the room toward bars, hors d'oeuvres, and the like.

- Have staffers keep an eye on the length of the waiting line. If things are moving too slowly, these helpers should relay a prearranged, subtle signal to speed up.

- Watch details. Because it is not proper to eat, drink, or smoke in a receiving line, locate tables or waiters with trays nearby so that guests can deposit plates, cups, or smoking materials before they reach the introducer.

- If the floor is not carpeted and you are concerned about people slipping, lay a skid-proof floor mat or carpet runner. Also, if many of your guests are older persons, consider providing seating by placing a small sofa or two in the area.

- Never assume a celebrity will stand in a receiving line. Such participation must be negotiated as part of his or her contract. If a celebrity does agree to take part, guests should not be permitted to ask for autographs as they go through the line.

• • •

How to Decide Who Sits Where

Seating a function can be the most tedious and frustrating aspect of the entire planning process. Invariably, no matter how far in advance you have planned, last-minute changes will still occur as guests are enjoying cocktails in the next room.

Every planner ultimately develops a system for assigning and rearranging seats. Some write names on colored slips of paper or on sticky notes; some use computer software. Regardless of how you match names with chairs, whether you are seating 1,000 people for a gala or 10 people for dinner at the president's home, there are some unbendable rules and some tricks of the trade every planner should know.

Seated at the Right Hand

The number-one rule is that the guest of honor be given a special place to sit. In contemporary etiquette, which is based on a person's rank or status, not gender, that spot is on the right-hand side of the host. The second-most-important guest is seated on the host's left. The third-most-important guest is seated to the cohost's right, and the fourth-most-important guest is on the cohost's left. The shape of the table is irrelevant to this order.

Generally Speaking

Each table should have a designated host. This person can be an administrator, a faculty member, or a volunteer, such as an alumni board member.

To complete the arrangement, determine who is the most prominent guest at the table, and seat him or her on the right side of the host. If at all possible, try to arrange guests man-woman-man-woman. In a business setting, it is now considered acceptable to seat husbands and wives together. This is based on the idea the couple is representing the organization as a team. Better than seating couples side-by-side, however, is to seat them at the same table but intermixed with other guests.

If you are hosting people who don't speak English, it is gracious to place someone who speaks their native language beside them.

Seating at Fund-Raising Events

Meet with development officers before seating a fund-raising event to determine who has purchased premium tickets that include priority seating. Decide whether there are people who need to be seated with certain individuals to facilitate cultivation efforts or if there are interpersonal or political issues that need to considered. For example, don't seat business rivals together. It is fine to place couples who are friends at the same table to ensure they have a good time. This is especially important in making newcomers feel at ease and ensuring that people will enjoy your fund raiser enough to return next year.

When arranging the placement of tables, be certain everyone who paid a premium for a good seat can see and hear equally well. Check top-level donor tables to be sure none has obstructed views, is positioned in front of a loudspeaker that will blast in guests' ears, or is so close to the stage that it is difficult to watch the action.

Under no circumstances should you fill empty places at premium-priced tables with staff members or with guests who have not paid to sit there. Instead, have the waiters clear any open place settings. Ideally, this should be done before guests enter the dining room so that adjustments can be made discreetly, but in practice it is safer to wait until the first course has been served to accommodate latecomers.

Seating by Rank

When you are entertaining foreign leaders, members of the diplomatic corps, members of Congress, state and local government officials, religious leaders, or members of the military, you must observe the rules of official protocol and seat guests according to their ranks.

In the complicated world of protocol (the rules that govern relations between governments) precedence and rank are very important. Disregarding them is a great offense to persons who are accustomed to abiding by them.

Stated in an oversimplified way, seating by precedence gives the best places to those at the top of an organization's hierarchy. The tricky part begins when you must mesh people from various organizations and determine who outranks whom.

On campus, the ranking administrator is the president or chancellor; next is the provost.

If you are not certain of a person's rank by looking at his or her title, telephone the organization for clarification.

To get help in seating by rank, consult a comprehensive etiquette book such as Letitia Baldrige's *New Complete Guide to Executive Manners* or *Protocol: The Complete Handbook of Diplomatic, Official and Social Usage* by Mary Jane McCaffree and Pauline Innis.

Tell 'Em Where to Go

Once your seating plan is complete, draw a seating chart and number each table. Display the numbers on the tables by using small metal stanchions made for this purpose. Make a blowup of the floor plan with the tables numbered, and display it on an easel outside the dining room.

As guests arrive, give each a small white "table card" (two by four inches) with his or her name written on the front and his or her assignment on the back. If cards are presented in a tiny envelope, write the guest's name on the outside as it appears on his or her place card. Another option is a larger card (three by 3 1/2 inches) that is folded in half. Write the guest's name on the outside and the table number on the inside.

Arrange the cards in alphabetical order on the registration table. By the time dinner is about to begin, a quick glance will tell you who has not shown up. This method is not foolproof, however, as some guests will bypass the registration table. Don't use table cards or numbers unless you have more than three tables.

Keep the dining-room doors closed until seating time to prevent guests from switching place cards or saving seats. Station staff members with alphabetical lists inside the dining room to help guide guests who can't find their tables. Other handy items for these staffers are copies of the seating chart and small flashlights. If the event is very large, provide staff members with walkie-talkies or cellular phones so that questions can be relayed and resolved quickly.

Contingency Plans

Have a fully set table waiting in the wings that can be moved into position at a moment's notice in case you have walk-in guests.

Keep a supply of blank place cards and table cards that can be lettered on the spot.

Fill empty seats with staff members if necessary.

The Dais

Amazingly, the dais party, the persons who are most honored and most on display during an event, are often seated incorrectly.

The dais (sometimes called the head table) is a place of honor for speakers, those being recognized, and official representatives of the host organization. If your event is underwritten by a corporation or foundation, it is proper to seat its representative on the dais as well.

If there is a lectern positioned in the center of the dais, the event host should be seated on its right as you face the audience. The guest of honor is seated on the host's right. The second-most-important guest is seated beside the lectern on its left, and the second host is seated to that person's left.

The remainder of the dais party is seated by alternating between the right and left sides of the table. The third most-important guest is seated on the right side with the third host; the fourth-most-important guest is on the left side with the fourth host, and so on.

If the dais party is large and you have more than one tier of tables and chairs, the most important people are seated on the lowest level, with the host and guest of honor in the center.

Spouses of dais guests should be assigned places at tables close to the dais for a good view and be seated beside table hosts who will be attentive to their needs.

It is acceptable to invite the spouse of the featured speaker to sit on the dais, but in truth, most would probably prefer to sit elsewhere. If you are in doubt, ask well in advance of the event.

Dais participants should process into the dining room after the other guests are seated. To orchestrate a grand entrance, designate a staff member or the emcee to make an announcement. The party should then process into the room to music. The audience should rise and applaud as they enter. (You may want to plant staff members to facilitate this.)

Proper Place Cards

Place cards help guests find their seats at tables and add a touch of elegance to both formal and informal gatherings.

For a formal occasion, place cards should be of stiff stock that is plain white or eggshell in color. It is acceptable for them to have a gilt or colored border or to have the institutional seal or other logo (such as a capital campaign symbol) embossed or printed at the top of the card. Cards that are otherwise decorated should not be used for a formal occasion.

The most correct way to complete the cards is to hand-letter them in black ink. Use only the guest's title or honorific and last name (Dr. Brown, Ms. Rogers). When two guests have the same last name, add first names for clarity (Ms. Diane Rogers, Ms. Tracy Rogers). Be certain the lettering is large and bold enough for people to read from a distance.

Persons who have rank or who are current or former elected officials must have their rank indicated before their names (Governor Black).

If the party is large or most guests are strangers, it is acceptable to use people's first and last names. When the party is small and guests know one another well, use first names only.

When places have been set with the folded napkin on top of the service plate, the place card belongs on top of the napkin. When the napkin is presented laying on the table top to the left of the forks, the place card goes above the service plate at the center of the place setting. (See Figure 4-1 on page 48).

It is never acceptable to rearrange place cards in order to secure a "better" seat.

• • •

What About Parking?

Parking is a problem whether events are held in city hotels, at civic buildings, or on campus. While definitely an unglamorous part of events management, parking is a guest's first impression and an important component of extending a gracious welcome. Parking problems can annoy guests and get events started on a sour note.

Parking Basics

Parking should be easily accessible, especially for night events. If the parking area or garage is too far away, arrange for a valet or shuttle-bus service. Be sure the lots have adequate security, both for guests' parked cars and for people walking to their cars. All parking areas should be well lighted and patrolled. Always reserve places for guests of honor, campus officials, and anyone else who is crucial to your program.

When using areas without marked parking places, such as a field or lawn, have people directing cars so that lines are straight, exits are clear, adequate driving lanes are available, and the maximum number of vehicles can be accommodated.

On campus, always provide free parking, even if it means building the costs into ticket prices and paying a lump sum from the event budget. Definitely provide

VIP parking for event sponsors, underwriters, and patrons as one of the perks that go with higher-priced tickets.

Consider the weather and how it will affect your parking arrangements; determine when the majority of people will want to leave; and check other events that may be happening on campus at the same time.

If you are reserving a parking lot for special use, post a notice a few days ahead so that people can make other arrangements. Secure the lots as early as possible to prevent unwanted parkers from filling spaces.

How many spaces will you need? As a general rule, figure 2 1/2 people per car. Remember to provide handicapped parking and emergency access lanes for fire or other emergency vehicles.

Campus security can advise you on your state's requirements.

Universal Hassle: Campus Parking

When planning an event on campus, meet with parking services or campus security early in the process. If you are sponsoring a large concert or festival in a convocation center or stadium, campus security will probably already have a plan for parking, lot security, and traffic dispersal. Critical to getting cars out of the lots is a plan that will enable traffic to flow away from the venue as quickly as possible. This can be accomplished by clearly marking exits, providing adequate signage indicating which lanes to use to connect with major highways, and, when necessary, making traffic one-way on key arteries. Campus security may also suggest stationing officers at the intersections of major roads in a two-block area to direct traffic and regulate traffic signals.

For smaller events, especially formal occasions, members of campus service clubs, athletic teams, or Greek organizations are usually happy to provide valet service in exchange for a contribution.

If you plan to use students or to hire valets, check with your risk-management office to determine any additional insurance needs. Meet with the valets before the event to discuss where and how to park the cars, what to wear, and when to report for work. Emphasize the need to respect the automobiles they will be driving. Establish a policy on tipping, and be sure the valets know and obey it.

If you create a shuttle service, use enough vehicles to minimize waiting, especially at peak times. All vans and shuttles should be free of charge and clearly marked. Provide each guest with information on routes, times, and stops.

Meet with shuttle drivers beforehand to review work schedules and routes and to discuss the event in detail. Review where to pick up passengers and how long to wait. Drivers will probably be your guests' first point of contact, and many visitors will ask them general questions. Leave activity schedules on each bus, and be certain the drivers are knowledgeable about not only the event but your campus as well and are willing to make a friendly impression.

Parking Garages and Paid Lots

Parking at public buildings like civic centers, theaters, music halls, and athletic stadiums is usually run by a different company from the one that manages the facility. Some rental contracts include parking, but in other cases it may be necessary to negotiate a separate parking agreement. If you don't want guests to pay for parking on arrival, make arrangements for vouchers or a lump payment based on the total number of cars parked.

At hotels that have private garages, negotiate parking as part of your rental contract, and try swapping parking for recognition in the event program, especially if the event is a fund raiser. (Parking is not deductible as a gift-in-kind because it is a service.)

If you are using a private country club or similar facility that has valet parking, negotiate the fees including a flat tip so that guests do not have to pay. If you want to offer VIPs special parking, arrange it in advance so that parking workers know where to direct cars.

Be Kind to the Neighbors

Unfortunately, efforts to make guests feel welcome can sometimes irritate neighbors and employees. At one university, staffers are periodically displaced from their regular parking places without notice to accommodate guests attending a quarterly seminar sponsored by the conferences office. On seminar mornings, traffic jams result in an already congested part of campus while angry regular parkers are turned away and forced to fend for themselves.

Another university's president's home is situated in an upscale neighborhood at the end of a cul-de-sac and lacks parking for all but a few cars. The home is frequently used for entertaining, and over the course of time neighbors grew weary of the eyesore and inconvenience of cars parked along the residential street. The neighbors got up a successful petition to prevent parking on the street. Cars are now valet parked at a lot several blocks away.

If event parking or traffic frequently impinges on your neighbors, try improving relations by sending them a friendly note and a schedule of major events before each semester begins. Plan a gathering just for them once a year to say thanks for being such good sports.

CHAPTER 4
Food and Beverage

• • •
Cocktails

Cocktail parties are a standard part of the campus events scene. They offer a less expensive alternative to hosting guests for dinner and serve as a pleasant way for people to network.

There are three types of cocktail parties: the simple stand-up cocktail hour at the end of the day; a cocktail buffet, which is longer and more formal; and the cocktail reception, which is formal and often held in the late evening.

An invitation for cocktails usually means people will stop by on their way home from work or en route to another function. Cocktails usually last one to 1 1/2 hours, beginning no earlier than 5 p.m. A cocktail invitation means drinks and hors d'oeuvres. Guests are expected to arrive within 20 minutes or so of the stated time, circulate to visit others, enjoy refreshments, and leave.

When a cocktail party precedes dinner, plan the hors d'oeuvres to be less filling and to complement the dinner menu. It is acceptable to shorten the length to 30 to 45 minutes, which is sufficient for all guests to arrive and get situated before being called to the dining room.

Sophisticated guests know not to carry their cocktails into the dining room. Provide small tables or stands in conspicuous places on the route to collect glasses. Regardless of your efforts, some people will insist on taking their drinks to the table with them, and there is little you can do to prevent it.

A cocktail buffet is an appropriate way to entertain before a theater or music performance, a lecture, or an art show opening. Cocktail buffets usually begin about 6 p.m. and last for two to three hours. The quantity and quality of foods offered should be a sufficient substitute for supper, and room setups should include places to sit down to eat. Never use the term "heavy hors d'oeuvres" to refer to this kind of party. Do not invite or expect performers or lecturers to attend cocktail functions before a performance. They need quiet, private time in order to prepare to perform their best.

A cocktail reception is a sophisticated, formal (sometimes black-tie) party held immediately before or after a performance or other event. A cocktail reception calls for the best of everything, including champagne. If it is held in the early evening, the menu consists of a sumptuous array of fancy cocktail foods and hot buffet items. If held after an event, add desserts to what becomes an elegant late-night supper. It is acceptable to invite performers to a cocktail reception when it is held after the show.

Cocktail Basics

Issue invitations to cocktail parties about three weeks ahead. Hire only trained bartenders. Serve the best brands you can afford in glasses, not plastic. (Use plastic if you are outdoors tailgating or in a picnic atmosphere.) Use high-quality, cocktail-size paper napkins embossed with your campus seal or in campus colors. If you are entertaining at the president's home, rent cloth cocktail napkins from a caterer or linen supply company.

Review with your bartenders the manner of service (serve beer and soda in glasses, please, not cans) and your policy on tipping. Request that bartenders wear a uniform appropriate to the occasion. Hire additional waiters to collect dirty plates and glasses, pass food, and serve drinks. Always offer an adequate and highly visible array of nonalcoholic beverages.

To avoid congestion, include several stations for food and beverages. Close the bar about a half-hour before the party ends to discourage people from lingering.

Work the Room

One of the main reasons for hosting a cocktail party is to facilitate friendships. Development officers, alumni personnel, and administrators need to be especially adept at working a room. This means knowing the purpose of the function, being familiar with the guest list, and skillfully joining and exiting conversation groups. No guest should leave the party without having been greeted several times by staff members.

Arriving guests should be greeted at the door by the host and hostess or ranking staff members (not student workers or low-level clerical staff). Without greeters, guests can wander in and around the party, anonymously grab a bite to eat, and slip away. Meanwhile, you have lost the reason for hosting them—to make personal contact.

During the event, it is the staff's responsibility to circulate constantly, making certain every guest feels welcome and keeping an eye out for problems (the buffet needs more plates, a spill needs to be cleaned up). All staff members should greet and thank the host and hostess. (Do this even when you are the event planner, and the host is your boss. You are thanking the host and hostess for taking their time to make your event a success.)

Staff members should not be allowed to congregate on the fringes of the event talking among themselves or gorging on buffet food. Staff members should limit their alcohol intake or drink nonalcoholic beverages while they are on duty.

• • •

Cash Bars

Cash bars are being offered at functions as a way of controlling costs because few institutions can afford to foot the bill for an open bar. Sometimes cash bars are unavoidable, but for the nicest events and most important guests, it is preferable to find another option that is more gracious and still affordable. Requiring guests to pay for their drinks at your party is awkward and not very classy. Instead, avoid the problem by eliminating the open bar and offering only wine and a nonalcoholic beverage before dinner. Work with your caterer to develop a hot beverage that will complement dinner. If you must rely on a cash bar, note it on the invitation so that guests come prepared with adequate funds.

Another reason for the proliferation of cash bars at campus events is the misconception that handling alcoholic beverages in this manner exonerates the planner, event host, and institution from social host liability laws and lawsuits. This is not true. The only certain protection from alcohol-related lawsuits is not to serve it at all. Depending on how they are set up, cash bars can actually bring more trouble—it is illegal in some states to sell drinks or tickets for drinks without a liquor license.

• • •

Which Wine, What Food?

Wondering which wine to serve with what food? Here is a basic guide to readily available, reasonably priced domestic wines suitable for most occasions. When the event demands something extra special, or if your guest of honor is a connoisseur, consult your chef or the proprietor of a good wine shop for advice.

The red wines listed here should be served at room temperature, the whites at 45 to 55 degrees. Lightly chill champagne by placing the bottles on ice. Sherry and port are served at room temperature.

Consult your chef or wine proprietor when choosing a wine to be served with salad. Many dressings, especially those heavily flavored with vinegar, garlic, or onion, compete with wine and should be considered before making a selection.

Serve these with hors d'oeuvres.

- **White wines:**
  Chardonnay, Chenin Blanc, Johannisberg Riesling, Sauvignon Blanc, White Zinfandel
- **Any champagne**
- **Red wines:**
  Merlot, Pinot Noir, Gamay Beaujolais

Serve these with pasta dishes with cream sauce or seafood.

- **White wines:**
  Chardonnay, Chenin Blanc, Johannisberg Riesling, Sauvignon Blanc
- **Any champagne**
- **Red wines:**
  Merlot or Pinot Noir

Serve these with beef or game.

- **Red wines:**
  Cabernet Sauvignon, Merlot, Pinot Noir, Zinfandel

Serve these with fowl, pork, or veal.

- **White wines:**
  Chardonnay, Johannisberg Riesling, Sauvignon Blanc, White Zinfandel
- **Any champagne**
- **Red wines:**
  Cabernet Sauvignon, Merlot, Pinot Noir, Zinfandel

Serve these with dessert.

Any champagne, Cream Sherry, port

• • •

Toasting

A toast is a special tribute to the person it honors. The sentiment expressed should be sincere and, ideally, create a personal link to the honoree. Because most people are not comfortable toasting, script the toast and practice it. It is best to avoid humor, which might fall flat or offend someone. Never use off-color jokes or profane words or relate potentially embarrassing stories. Toasts can be drunk with either wine or water; it is the gesture that has meaning.

There are two traditional types of toast:

1. *A welcoming toast at the beginning of the meal.* The host or hostess remains seated and gives a toast to welcome everyone. (This is why the savvy guest doesn't take a sip of wine until the host or hostess does.)

2. *A toast to the guest of honor at the beginning of the dessert course.* This toast is made by the host or hostess. (The signal that this kind of toast will be made is the presence of a champagne glass.)

Here are some toasting dos and don'ts:

- The host has the right and privilege of making the first toast.
- The person proposing the toast stands. (Exception: If it is a welcoming toast, the person remains seated.)
- On a formal occasion, everyone but the person being toasted should rise.
- The person receiving the toast remains seated. The person being honored

does not raise a glass or take a drink. (This would be toasting oneself and is never done.)

- A toast should be brief (one minute or less).
- The person who has been honored is obligated to return the toast, either immediately or after a brief amount of time; never wait until the end of the meal. (An appropriate response is a brief salute to the host, a thank-you for the hospitality, and a comment about the occasion.)
- It is not necessary to clink glasses together. Simply raising glasses is sufficient.
- Toasts can be given by either a man or woman.
- It is acceptable to incorporate famous sayings or quotes from poems as long as they are in keeping with the occasion and in good taste.
- If a host has not offered a toast and a guest desires to do so, he or she should discreetly ask the host's permission first. ("Would you mind if I proposed a toast?")
- To toast at a cocktail reception, wait until the crowd seems to be at its peak.

• • •

Presenting Food

Serving food to a guest is as symbolic as it is practical. In our culture, food is a way of offering friendship. Each time we serve our guests, we are offering a kind of gift. As events planners, part of our responsibility is to ensure that the food is delicious, plentiful, and properly and beautifully presented.

• • •

Coffee, Tea, and Soda

Coffee breaks are an integral part of meetings, but often, the presentation is given little or no thought. Because the coffee cart may be one of the first impressions guests receive, make the impression a good one. Coffee service should be beautifully arranged on a linen-covered table with a bouquet of fresh flowers. Set it up outside of the meeting room so that it is not a constant distraction to the proceedings. Choices should include fresh, hot coffee (both regular and decaffeinated), hot water for tea (offer a variety of flavored and plain teas in bags displayed in an attractive wooden box or similar container), and a selection of juices. In the afternoon, bottled water and soda can be added.

- Serve milk or half-and-half in small pitchers, not in little plastic tubs.
- Use china cups and saucers and metal teaspoons, not disposable plastic spoons or stir sticks.
- Place sugar loose in a pretty bowl with a sugar spoon, or offer cubes and serve with tongs. Artificial sweetener is served in individual packets. Place the packets in an attractive bowl, preferably one that matches or at least complements the sugar bowl.
- Offer paper-thin slices of lemon for tea.

- Provide high-quality, paper napkins.
- If you are serving rolls, bagels, pastries, or fruit, provide luncheon-size plates. You'll also need knives, forks, and butter. (Serve pretty butter balls or piped shapes, not paper-covered butter pats.)
- Always provide glasses for cold beverages so that people don't have to drink from a bottle or can. Provide a container for ice and serving tongs so that guests needn't shovel ice with a glass.
- Provide a place nearby for people to deposit their used cups and dishes. This area should be close to the break service but not positioned where guests see it as they are serving themselves. Place a nice-looking trash receptacle close by but away from the food. Attendants should quickly remove dirty dishes and litter so that the break area always looks fresh. Replace soiled linen before the next break.

• • •

Casual Events

The casual entertaining associated with student orientations, tailgating, alumni reunions, and similar events constitutes a large part of a planner's year. Casual events should reflect the same attention to detail and personal style that the most elegant function draws. Casual events can easily be raised from the mundane to the classy with a few simple changes. What's more, casual events often generate mounds of nonrecyclable waste, much of it plastic-and much of which can be avoided. Caterers like the convenience of serving foods in wrapped and packaged individual servings, but getting rid of all that packaging not only makes foods look more appealing, it makes sense ecologically.

Give casual events a more gracious touch in these ways:

- Avoid paper napkins, condiments wrapped in paper and plastic, and those ubiquitous plastic bags filled with plastic silverware. Replace with stainless-steel utensils wrapped in a cloth napkin (inexpensive bandannas work great), and offer condiments from shakers or other containers.
- Serve on reusable dishes, in small baskets, or on paper plates instead of plastic or Styrofoam plates.
- Ask caterers not to put plastic wrap on sandwiches, cookies, silverware, and condiments.
- Offer chips and snacks in baskets, not individual bags.
- If you are concerned about keeping food protected, serve lunch in a recyclable box, or keep foods from drying out by covering with cloths until serving time.
- Serve soda and beer in glasses so that guests don't have to drink from a can. If you must use disposable cups, choose wax-coated instead of Styrofoam.
- Inspect the serving containers and utensils the caterer plans to use. Beat-up, shopworn items should not be allowed on a buffet in sight of the guests. If your caterer or campus food service simply doesn't have anything nicer, purchase your own and keep them for use at your parties.

• • •

Buffets

Perhaps the most important aspect of serving a buffet is to consider its location carefully in relation to access needed by the caterers and the number of guests who must go through the line. Nobody wants to stand in line waiting for dinner because poor positioning of the table or arrangement of foods and utensils has created a bottleneck. For a large crowd that will arrive all at once, provide more than one serving table, serve from both sides of the table, or both.

Arrange and decorate the table so that it is a feast for all the senses. Many caterers are especially good at this and can create decorations to interpret your theme. Insist on clean, stain-free linen that is not faded. Battered pans, beat-up bowls, and institutional serving utensils are not allowed. Plates should be warm and dry, not still covered with water droplets from the dishwasher. Avoid overloading the buffet to point that it appears wasteful.

Arrange foods in logical order. Plates should come first, then the main course. Next are side dishes, salads, and finally, rolls. Present dessert on a separate table or in a different room. It much easier for your guests if flatware and napkins are placed at their tables and if drinks are served to them by waiters. Most people struggle to manage one plate in a buffet line; it's even harder to hold a beverage, fill several plates, and pick up flatware.

Once guests are seated and beverages served, waiters are needed to clear plates and direct guests to dessert. Serve guests who cannot go through the line because of physical difficulties; offer to accompany a guest who needs assistance and prepare a plate according to his or her wishes.

Insist that food be kept piping hot. Foods that appear to have sat too long on the steam table should be replaced. Serving vessels should be replenished in the kitchen out of sight of the guests. Food should never be scraped from one container to another at the buffet table. Provide an ample supply of plates so that guests can have a clean one on each visit to the buffet.

Hosting a buffet does not release you from the obligation to provide a comfortable, beautiful spot at which to enjoy eating. Prepare tables with centerpieces in the same manner you would for a served meal. For those occasions when tables are simply not an option, at least provide seating for everyone so that no one has to stand. I once saw a vice president's wife covered with a guest's hot spaghetti dinner because of lack of seating. Because it was impossible to eat her own helping of the slippery stuff standing up, she sat down on the floor. An unwary passing guest tripped on her and dumped his food right in her lap.

• • •

Served Meals

Whether you are serving a casual supper of hot soup and sandwiches before an evening hockey game or an elegant black-tie dinner to announce the start of a capital campaign, high-quality and correct service should be your hallmark. In the crowded and competitive world of events, distinguishing yours from others can be as simple (and inexpensive) as becoming a stickler for detail and giving your events the flair that comes from doing things properly on every occasion.

• • •

The Table

Tables so crowded together that waiters must squeeze to pass by and chairs jammed so tightly that people can barely move their arms to eat are two of the most common mistakes at large campus events. While most planners use formulas to determine how many tables are needed to accommodate guests, common sense would often be a better guide. Even though a table might be designed to seat 10 people, whether or not they will be comfortable depends on everything from the width of the chairs to what is being served. Seating 10 people per table for a six-course dinner with lots of stemware and flatware will create a crowded, cluttered look and a less-than-delightful dining experience. In such cases, limiting seating to eight persons per table would be much more comfortable for diners and waiters.

When in doubt, arrange to have a test table set up. Is there enough room to move without bumping the person next to you? Can you easily reach glasses without fear of knocking something over? A good rule of thumb is to allow 24 inches per place setting, 30 inches if there are lots of courses and stemware. The extra space is not only appreciated by guests, it allows servers to do their jobs in the most professional manner.

The same is true for the number of tables that can fit into a ballroom. Particularly when guests are older or in formal attire, it is much more considerate to limit seating, remove some tables, and leave ample room for people to maneuver in between. No one enjoys eating with his or her chairback bumping one at the table behind. If you want additional spacing for place settings or between tables, specify it when you make arrangements.

Round tables are always preferable, and they are mandatory (rent them if necessary) for formal occasions. Every campus planner must, however, occasionally deal with rectangular tables. When this is the case, limit seating to the sides (avoid the ends because the legs are in the way).

• • •

Chairs

Banquet chairs take a beating. For function after function, they are stacked, dragged out, and stacked again. Seats become stained, food particles stick in the space between seat and frame, and legs warp or wobble. Insist on the nicest chairs available, and check them all before each event. Chairs vary greatly in the pitch of the back, angle of the seat, and height from the floor. Sit in the chairs you have selected at the tables you plan to use to learn whether the seat will be comfortable for dining. For the most special functions, consider renting upgraded chairs, or rent chair covers from a linen-supply company.

• • •

Tablescapes

There are books written on how to create a beautiful tabletop scene. One designer says the table merits the most planning attention because it becomes a guest's "private space" during the function and is where he or she will spend the majority of time. Therefore, make the space comfortable and pleasant to view.

A classy presentation begins long before flowers are ordered or a theme is interpreted with props. Linen, flatware, dishes, and accessories like salt and pepper shakers must be in first-rate condition. No guest should ever have the experience of picking up a cup to expose a hole in the tablecloth. Inspect all tables before guests arrive, and insist that dingy, stained, or torn linen be replaced and chipped dishes or bent flatware be removed. Your high standards will soon be noted, and savvy caterers will become more watchful of the things they use for your events.

When choosing centerpieces, bear in mind the purpose of the event, and don't be afraid to scale back proposals from florists if they seem too flamboyant for the occasion. (How much do you want your donors to think you've spent on flowers?) To facilitate conversation, it is best to avoid four-foot-tall centerpieces and mounds of greenery that people can't see around. Centerpieces can be creative and composed from things other than flowers. They need not be expensive, and decorations can vary from table to table.

Candles

Candles add beauty and serenity to any table. They can be a real friend to university events planners because they are inexpensive, lend themselves to a variety of containers, and are readily available. There are no hard rules about the placement or number of candles other than that formal occasions require new white tapers. Candles should not be used during the daytime; save them instead for evening functions. Light candles before guests enter the dining room, and keep them lit until the guests have departed. If candles are providing the only light, you will need approximately one per person to supply adequate illumination; otherwise, figure two to four candles for each table of eight. Never use scented candles on dining tables.

Before developing a tablescape that relies on candles, check whether fire laws permit their use in your facility. Local laws vary, and some communities don't permit candles at all. Others require that the flame be enclosed in a fireproof container such as a hurricane shade.

Napkins

Caterers are fond of creating fanciful folds with napkins. This is acceptable, and a beautifully folded napkin can add a creative element to your tablescape. Steer away from napkins stuffed in goblets because they are top-heavy and can be awkward to remove. It is acceptable to use napkin rings or to tie ribbons on napkins for all but the most formal occasions.

Dinner napkins range in size from 22 to 30 inches square. Luncheon napkins are smaller, ranging in size from 14 to 24 inches square. For the most formal occasions, use the traditional soft rectangle fold, and place the napkin in the center of the service plate. If the first course has been preset, or the meal is informal and no service plate is used, place the napkin on the table to the left of the forks. Never place napkins under forks. Paper napkins are acceptable for coffee breaks, cocktails, and very casual gatherings like a barbecue or tailgating. Never use them for a buffet, served meal, or fancy reception.

Place Cards

Place cards belong in the center of the plate on top of the napkin. If that position is impractical, put the cards on the table centered above the plate. Decorative cards or cards in fanciful holders are acceptable for all but the most formal occasions. Read about proper dimensions and how to write place cards in Chapter 3 on Receiving Guests.

Menu Cards

Menu cards aren't often seen at university events, but they do add an extra-special touch to the occasion. Menu cards are meant to be taken home as a souvenir. On campus, this function is sometimes now filled by souvenir programs that list the menu. Menu cards are appropriate at only the most formal dinners and should be white or ecru stock, about 4-1/2 inches by 6-1/2 inches tall. The stock must match the place cards.

Print the card on the vertical. The campus seal or event logo can be used at the top; lettering should be in black ink, either handwritten or printed. Put the date of the dinner in the upper right corner and the word "dinner" in the center. If there is a guest of honor, that person's name can be added.

Dinner
Honoring
Person's Name

List the food and wines in English. If the food and wines are of foreign origin, the native language can be used on menu cards. It is the host's prerogative to decide which to use. Don't list accompaniments like relishes, rolls, jams, fruit, chocolates, tea, water, or coffee. Make one card for every two guests, and place the card flat on the table to the left of the forks or centered above the place setting behind the dessert spoon and fork. It is also acceptable to lean the card against a glass. If you have menu-card holders, and they are of a design that is consistent with the occasion, use them.

Table Numbers

The stanchions that hold table numbers belong near the center of the table positioned so that they are easily read. Turn the numbers to face the direction from which most people will enter the room, and use lettering that is large enough to be read from a distance. Waiters remove the stanchions and numbers as soon as guests are seated.

Salt and Pepper Shakers

A pair of salt and pepper shakers for every two guests should be placed on the table. Caterers often do not own nice-looking shakers, but under no circumstances should you settle for clunky shakers that look as if they belong in a cafeteria. Instead, invest in your own supply of small, matching glass shakers for your events. When salt and pepper shakers are used at *each* place, they go on the left side of the setting, just above and slightly to the right of the bread plate. The salt shaker belongs on the left side of the pair, slightly in front of the pepper shaker. When a pair of shakers are shared, they belong between the two place settings, slightly below the stemware. The pepper shaker goes on the left, slightly behind the salt.

● ● ●

Table Settings

There are many comprehensive etiquette books that discuss flatware and stemware and their uses. When in doubt, always consult a reference. What is most important for special events planners to memorize is the basic correct arrangement of utensils at the table (see Figure 4-1). Many caterers or their setup crews do not know the correct placement of flatware and stemware, or they use a hybrid setting because they like the way it looks. Always check the tables before guests arrive.

If you are seated at the table, the plate belongs at the center of your place. Knives and spoons belong on your right side, forks on the left. A bread plate should always be used. It goes on the left side in the 11-o'clock position. Wine glasses are arranged on the right side at approximately the one- and two-o'clock positions. The water goblet goes at about the one-o'clock position, directly above the blade of the knife that is closest to the dinner plate (this could be the dinner or salad knife, depending on the courses being served).

Wine glasses do not have to be arranged in a straight line. Instead, group them according to use. If white wine is served first, put the white-wine glass in the lowest position so that it can be reached without knocking over another glass. The red wine goes slightly behind it, and the champagne flute belongs at the back of the grouping, as it is the tallest and will be used last (for the dessert toast). When coffee is served, the cup belongs on the right side at about the four-o'clock position.

Flatware is arranged so that the utensils needed for the first course are farthest away from the plate. Knife blades point in toward the plate. If dessert forks and spoons are at the place setting, they appear immediately above the plate. The tines of the dessert fork point to the right of the place setting, and the bowl of the dessert spoon points toward the left. The butter spreader rests across the top quarter of the bread plate, blade facing in toward the diner, with the handle end on the right or closest to the center of the place setting.

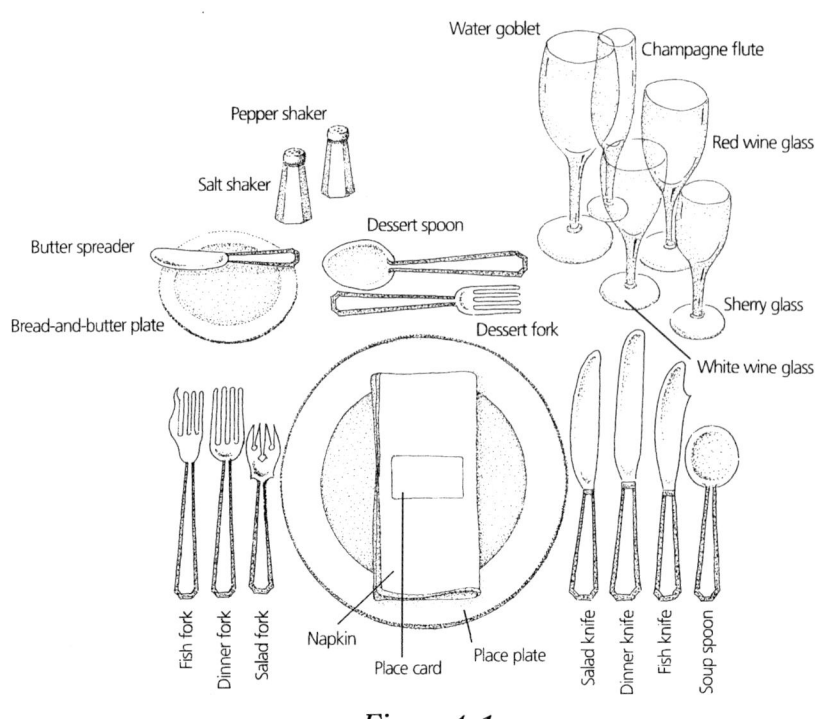

Water goblet

Champagne flute

Pepper shaker

Red wine glass

Salt shaker

Dessert spoon

Butter spreader

Bread-and-butter plate

Dessert fork

Sherry glass

White wine glass

Fish fork

Dinner fork

Salad fork

Napkin

Place card

Place plate

Salad knife

Dinner knife

Fish knife

Soup spoon

Figure 4-1.

The napkin belongs on top of the place plate (sometimes called a charger or service plate) or on the table at left of the forks. Avoid fancy folded napkins stuffed in wine or water goblets.

The place card (if used) goes on top of the napkin when the napkin is presented on top of the service plate. Otherwise, the place card should go at the center of the place setting, above the dessert fork and spoon.

• • •

Teach Students to Provide First-Class Service

A glass of milk was one student waiter's solution to a banquet guest's request for coffee cream. "I couldn't find the cream pitchers," he explained as he plunked the glass before the astonished man.

On another occasion, "we don't have that brand" was a student waiter's reply to a guest's request for a "light Scotch."

Grooming a polished corps of well-trained student waiters to serve banquets and events throughout the year is an important component of institutional image and can pay worthwhile public relations dividends. Often, waiters are the only representatives of the student body with whom campus guests interact. Their appearance, the manner in which they perform their duties, and the level of sophistication (or lack of it) they convey to alumni, donors, and friends are a direct reflection of your institution's image.

Recruit Doers

The first step toward building a top-flight team of student workers is to be selective at hiring time. One planner chooses "high energy go-getters" and looks for students who are majoring in hospitality fields, such as hotel management, recreation, or public relations. Next, she explores whether the applicant has the energy and time to do the job. If something else is a priority (an extra-heavy academic load or the desire to go home on weekends), she keeps looking.

Another planner asks candidates how they would handle hypothetical situations in order to determine their flexibility, ability to deal with multiple demands, and willingness to accommodate a diversity of people and beliefs.

Provide Training

Adequate training after hiring is essential. Begin by holding mandatory training sessions for all staff. This is the time to share your philosophy on customer service, your office mission statement, and your policy-and-procedures manual. Help students buy in to their role in making events successful by explaining the public relations and fund-raising functions of special events. Be certain they are well informed about general campus information such as the location of buildings, important happenings (such as the date of the big football rivalry game), and the basics of campus structure (how many colleges there are, the names of key administrators, how long the institution has been open).

Stress professional appearance and behavior, and be very specific about what clothing or uniforms students are allowed to wear on the job. A good standard outfit is black pants for men, black skirts for women, with long-sleeved white shirts. Black bow ties add a polished touch and can be worn by men or women.

All waiters should have uniforms that are clean and pressed, appropriate footwear, clean hands and fingernails, and a neat hairdo. Men should be clean-shaven. Jewelry should be minimal and small enough that it will not drag in the food or catch on stemware. Request that ornaments worn in unusual body piercings such as lips, eyebrows, nose, or tongue not be displayed while on duty.

Teach Proper Service

It is important to teach the basics of proper table service. Even if students have previous waitstaff experience, teach them the way you want things done during a hands-on training workshop. These standards become your style that will be used for all events. By communicating the importance of proper service and by teaching techniques to everyone at the same time, you create a shared pool of information, eliminate lots of future questions, and create a built-in safeguard because students can reinforce each other if procedural questions arise. Students who join the staff later should not be permitted to work until they, too, complete training. Team up with your catering manager to present a fun training session by teaching the basics, then dividing into teams and having students take turns serving one another.

Here are the basics of good service that all waiters should follow:

- The guest on the host's right (the guest of honor) is served first.

- Service continues around the table counterclockwise.
- The host is served last.
- The waiter presents the food from the diner's left side.
- Plates are removed from the diner's right side.
- Wine and other beverages are served and removed from the right side.
- Plates should be removed one per hand, never scraped and stacked in the presence of guests.
- No plates should be removed until everyone at the table is finished with the course.
- All plates and flatware pertaining to a course should be removed before the next course is served.
- Before dessert is served, all items from previous courses should be removed. This includes condiments, salt and pepper shakers, and bread and butter plates.
- Remove crumbs from the table with a linen napkin and a clean plate before dessert is served.
- Do not allow dirty dishes to remain in the dining area where guests can see them.
- Waitstaff should not engage in unnecessary conversation with guests.

At large events when speed is a consideration and each table may not have a host, service should begin with a woman and proceed counterclockwise. It is acceptable to serve from more than one side of the table simultaneously. Waiters should avoid rushing and instead take time to place the plates carefully before guests.

Give and Take Feedback

Some simple but important techniques will help retain student employees and make their work experience more meaningful:

- Show by example that you are a professional and expect professionalism in return. Give constructive criticism in private, and refresh standards taught in training as soon as skills begin to slip.
- Establish a chain of command by recruiting students to serve as captains who in turn provide direction for their peers. Be certain instructions between you and the captains are clearly given and understood.
- Be open to students' suggestions and feedback, and let them know it is okay to ask questions.
- Give frequent recognition for good performance, and remember to thank students personally for a job well done each time they work.

CHAPTER 5

Academic Traditions

*A*CADEMIC CEREMONIES GAIN MUCH OF their dignity and beauty from the traditional, stately march of faculty and academic officers that begins and concludes virtually every major occasion on the academic calendar. An academic procession is a kaleidoscope of black robes, colored hoods, beautiful banners, special music, and precious symbols. Its roots extend to the 12th century, when the church governed schools in Paris, and civil officials governed universities in Bologna. Today's academic costumes, class rings, and ceremonial objects are direct descendants of the symbols of office used by medieval scholars and civil authorities.

• • •

Academic Dress

Students began wearing caps and gowns in medieval times because gowns were the attire required by the church and because of the need to stay warm in unheated buildings. Patterned after monks' robes, the earliest academic robes were made of heavy wool. Over time, academic robes evolved to signify degree and rank.

The beautiful hoods that today indicate master's degrees began as humble cowls that could be attached to a gown and slipped over the head for warmth. This unique costume was also used to set students apart from townspeople, and some say this was the origin of the division in "town and gown" relations we still know today.

Mortarboards, or "oxford caps," trace their history to the square cap with a tuft on top that was awarded to students in the Middle Ages when they completed their courses of study and were recognized as "masters." The distinctive cap was a sign to all that the person had attained this status. Another part of the awarding of a degree, or mastership, was the presentation of a gold ring. Both cap and ring were presented during a public ceremony or convocation conducted by the school's faculty when a candidate had satisfactorily completed a course of study.

Prior to the Civil War, students at most American universities wore caps and gowns every day. By the end of the 19th century, colleges and universities were developing so many different academic costumes that a commission was formed by the American Council on Education to study the situation and make recommendations for a uniform code for academic regalia. In 1896, a standard code was adopted that is still followed today.

Gowns

According to the code, gowns are always black, although recently some institutions have started to create their own colorful robes for Ph.D. graduates.

Bachelor's Degree

The bachelor's gown falls to the knee, has long sleeves, and is worn closed in front and without a hood. It has no color or adornment.

Master's Degree

Modern master's gowns are like bachelor's gowns but have long, pointed sleeves. Traditional master's gowns feature a peculiar sleeve that requires the wearer to poke the arms out through a slit at the elbow. The rest of the sleeve dangles to about the knee. The sleeves end in a square bottom into which a semicircle has been cut.

Both styles are correct, and in either case the gown may be worn open or closed. Some institutions have begun adding colored bindings or knots of embroidery to indicate academic discipline. A master's gown is worn with a hood.

Ph.D.

The doctoral gown is the most elaborate. It is fuller, falls to ankle length, and is distinguished by flowing sleeves with three bars of velvet and a facing of velvet down the front. The bars and facing may be in black or the color of the faculty in which the degree was awarded. Doctoral gowns are traditionally worn open, but either open or closed is acceptable.

Some doctor's gowns are now awarded in the color of the university. If so, the sleeve bands are black or the color of the discipline. In this case, the doctor may chose to not wear a hood.

Ceremonial Gowns

University presidents and marshals typically wear special ceremonial gowns. These are long and flowing like a doctoral gown but are usually created in the institution's colors. Often, marshals wore ceremonial gowns with a fanciful headdress. The president's gown may be tailored to showcase the campus medallion, lavaliere, or collar. Some institutions incorporate the ceremonial gown into presidential installation ceremonies by removing the new president's own gown and dressing him or her in the new ceremonial robe.

Hoods

Hoods, most commonly presented today to master's-degree recipients, are very symbolic and beautiful. The hood is lined with a colored fabric, usually velvet, that indicates the college or university from which the wearer earned the degree. Many also use beautiful combinations of chevrons, bars, checks, crosses, tartans, or lozenges to show the institution's second color. The color patterns and order of their placement are adapted from classical heraldry. Finally, the hood's border or edge is outlined in a color that indicates the wearer's field of study.

The size of the hood also indicates degree. A bachelor's-degree hood (rarely seen anymore) is the smallest. It is usually black and hangs three feet down the wearer's back. The colored border is two inches wide. A master's-degree hood is 3 1/2 feet long with a three-inch-wide colored border. The doctor's hood is the largest at four feet long with five-inch-wide colored borders.

Caps

The mortarboard is always black and can be made of any suitable fabric. Velvet mortarboards are reserved for Ph.D.s. Some doctors wear a soft tam or a large beret after the style of those worn at Cambridge University. The mortarboard should be worn level on the head, not pushed back, so that the tassel falls in a line perpendicular to the ground.

Tassels

Tassels are attached to the button on the top of the mortarboard and can be black to indicate any degree or the color of the graduate's field of study. Tassels are usually quite long and dangle along the side of the wearer's face. Many institutions follow the tradition of having new graduates switch their tassels from the right side to the left after the degree is conferred. In fact, the tassel may properly be worn on either side.

Doctors and the governing officials of institutions have the right to wear tassels of golden threads. These are short, usually cut to hang about 2 1/2 inches over the edge of the cap or mortarboard. Most people sew the tassel in place for convenience.

• • •

Faculty Colors

Colors were assigned to academic disciplines and standardized for the first time in the United States in the late 19th century when the Intercollegiate Commission met to adopt a code of academic dress. The colors chosen had traditional meanings. Green was selected for medicine because it is the color of healing herbs. Red was the traditional color of the church and was therefore assigned to theology. Science was given golden yellow to signify the wealth of knowledge produced by research.

Revisions were made to the code in 1932, 1959, and, most recently, 1986 by the American Council on Education's Committee on Academic Costumes and Ceremonies. Otherwise, the code stands as it was written more than 100 years ago.

The following list represents the committee's list of faculty colors. On the subject of adding colors to represent new fields of study, the committee said, ". . .the fundamental guidelines of the academic costume code may be adapted to local conditions. Such adaptations are entirely acceptable as long as they are reasonable and faithful to the spirit of the traditions which give rise to the code. They are not acceptable when they further subdivide the recognized disciplines and designate new colors for such subdivisions. Problems may arise with emerging broad interdisciplinary areas; it is recommended that these be resolved by using the color of the discipline most nearly indicative of the new area."

Academic disciplines, or faculties, are symbolized by the following colors:

Agriculture	maize
Arts, letters, and humanities	white
Business	drab
Dentistry	lilac
Economics	copper
Education	light blue
Engineering	orange
Fine arts and architecture	brown
Forestry	russet
Journalism	crimson
Law	purple
Library science	lemon yellow
Medicine	green
Music	pink
Nursing	apricot
Oratory (speech)	silver gray
Pharmacy	olive green
Philosophy	dark blue
Physical education	sage green
Public Administration, including foreign service	peacock blue
Public health	salmon pink
Science	golden yellow
Social work	citron yellow
Theology	scarlet
Veterinary science	gray

• • •

Symbols of Office

Symbols or articles of office are highly symbolic and important parts of academic ceremonies. Symbols typically include a mace, a medallion or lavaliere, and treasured artifacts such as the institution's charter or original seal.

Mace

The mace is the symbol of the legal and chartered authority of the people—usually the president and vice presidents—to whom the trustees have delegated authority. When the mace is present, the authority of the university is present. When it leaves, the authority leaves, too. For this reason, the mace is brought into the gathering immediately before the governing body, usually the trustees and president.

A mace is almost always a custom-made piece of art and is often crafted from historic campus relics. A mace is usually decorated with gems and precious metals, often in the campus colors, and each component of the design is symbolic.

In the Middle Ages, the mace was a war club carried by a bodyguard to defend a person of authority. Today, its purpose is strictly ceremonial, and carrying it is a great honor reserved for a distinguished faculty member, an outstanding student, or the university marshal. During a ceremony, the mace rests on a velvet pillow or a specially made freestanding or tabletop holder. It should not be laid on the floor.

Medallion

Medallions, sometimes referred to as collars or lavalieres, often depict a campus's official seal and are typically set with gems. They are worn as part of a president's regalia on ceremonial occasions such as commencements or convocations. Some institutions give each president a medallion to keep; others pass along one medallion, engraving each president's name and years of tenure on the back.

Other Symbols

Symbols aren't always precious metals and gems. Some institutions use rare books, historic keys, maps, wills, tankards, and ancient chairs in academic ceremonies. If you don't have a showcase full of historic sterling-silver ceremonial items that have been handed down through the centuries, don't despair. A mace and medallion can be commissioned from an alumnus or art-faculty member. Symbols of office can be created by selecting items that relate to your mission or history. For example, an orb could be used to signify international programs. Or consider creating a link to the cultural heritage of your region. In Hawaii, traditional native symbols, including Kukui nuts and a Royal Ilima lei made of the tiny petals of an orange flower reserved for the most special occasions, were incorporated into a recent presidential inauguration.

Batons

Carried by the marshals of the colleges, batons are symbols of the bearers' authority as officers of protocol. Today, marshals are essentially ushers, but in medieval times, they were disciplinary officers. The baton each carries is, in essence, a miniature mace or war club. At a university, each college or school has its own baton crafted in fine wood and set with either the university seal or some decorative element that incorporates the color of the academic discipline.

Academic Seal

An academic seal is the official mark of an institution and is normally used on diplomas and other documents, displayed on the campus banner, and incorporated in the design of a mace or president's medallion. Most seals are round; many have a motto inscribed in Latin or English and depict scenes of discovery, teaching, cultural heritage, or a campus landmark.

The seal can be enlarged to be displayed as a piece of art, rendered on a high-quality banner, made into an emblem that attaches to a podium, or even recreated in flowers. Regardless of how it is presented, the seal makes an attractive impression and imparts an air of officiality wherever it is displayed. At some campuses, a person carries the seal in the procession.

Most universities have guidelines for the reproduction and display of the seal to ensure a consistent image and discourage disrespectful uses. The president's or public relations office is usually the source for these guidelines, which will likely include rules about size, placement on a page, correct ink colors, and disallowed uses. Because the seal is an official symbol of the university, it should be used judiciously and with dignity. It should not be stamped on T-shirts, souvenir items, and disposable cups and plates the way athletic logos or slogans might be.

Academic Banners

Colorful banners, called gonfalons, signifying a university's colleges and sometimes its student organizations contribute greatly to the pageantry and beauty of academic processions. Probably the closest similar display with which most Americans are familiar is the procession of country delegations during the opening ceremonies of the Olympic games. On campus, banners of the colleges and schools are in the colors traditionally associated with their discipline. Each banner is marched in at the head of the delegation from that college and posted near its seating area during the ceremony.

At some institutions, international students carrying flags from their homelands join processions on occasions like commencements or inaugurations.

Only a trained color guard, such as one from a campus ROTC unit, should present the U.S. flag. The flag should never be presented by a person in academic regalia. It is very important to observe the rules of flag etiquette for the display of the U.S. and international flags.

Displaying the U.S. Flag

Here is basic protocol for displaying the Stars and Stripes on U.S. soil:

- The U.S. flag is always afforded the place of honor. If you are standing on the stage facing the audience, the U.S. flag belongs on your right. The flags of your state and campus should be displayed on your left.
- To display the U.S. flag with a group of state flags, place all the flags in a row with the U.S. flag in the center. It should be elevated on a platform so that it is higher than all the others.

- When displaying the U.S. flag with flags of several other countries, arrange them in alphabetical order. All flags should be the same size and on separate poles that are the same height. (International law forbids the display of one flag above another.) Place all the flags in a straight line. Give the American flag the position of honor, and arrange the foreign flags to the left of it. On U.S. soil, the American flag should be the first one hoisted and the last one lowered.
- If the U.S. flag is displayed with the flag of one other country, the American flag, as the host flag, goes in the position of honor to the right of the foreign flag.
- When hanging the flag flat on a wall, the stars should be at the top. Either horizontally or vertically, the stars belong in the upper left-hand corner as you are facing the flag. When hanging flat behind a speaker's platform, the flag should be straight behind and above the speaker.
- To display the U.S. flag on the same pole with your state and institutional flags, the proper order is this: U.S. flag at the top, state flag in the middle, institutional flag lowest.
- In a procession, the American flag goes on the marching right. For example, if a color guard is presenting the United States and one other flag, and you are facing the guard, the American flag would be on your left-hand side. If several flags are being presented, line the flag bearers up shoulder to shoulder. The person carrying the U.S. flag should be positioned in the center of the line and march a step or two ahead of the others.
- When the flag is presented, the audience should stand.
- When "The Star-Spangled Banner" is played, it is most correct for a civilian to stand at attention with his or her right hand over the heart, although it is acceptable to simply face the flag or the direction of the music and stand at attention. Men should remove hats.
- The flag may not be used to cover or drape a lectern, table, platform, ceiling, or vehicle.
- Worn, torn, faded, or stained flags should be replaced.

• • •

Who Does What?

Many people performing many different roles characterize an academic procession. It is not uncommon to have as many as 1,000 marchers in a single procession. Before discussing the order of march, it might be helpful to review the cast of characters and the roles they perform.

Dais Party

Dais means "throne," and thinking of it this way makes it easy to remember that the dais is the seat of honor. The dais is an elevated platform at the front of the room and the stage on which the ceremony is conducted.

Who exactly constitutes the dais party varies from ceremony to ceremony, but membership is reserved for eminent persons whose participation is critical to the occasion.

The president is always seated on the dais. The mace precedes the entrance of the dais party as a signal that the authority of the institution is present. It is preferable from a logistical point of view to keep the dais party as small as possible. Prominent individuals who are not participating in the ceremony should be escorted to VIP seating in the front row of the assembly.

Delegates of Learned Societies and Scientific and Cultural Institutions

Persons who represent learned societies traditionally march in processions for historic convocations (such as an anniversary celebration) and presidential investiture ceremonies. Learned societies include Phi Beta Kappa, Phi Kappa Phi, the National Academy of Sciences, the American Historical Association, the American Philosophical Association, and the like. Representatives of these societies march in the order of their organization's founding, with the oldest going first. If the occasion is a presidential investiture, most of the societies sending delegates will be related to the president's field of scholarship.

Delegates Representing Other Universities and Colleges

When the academic universe was smaller, the installation of a new president or the opening of a new college or university was major news. By tradition, such occasions were celebrated by inviting representatives from every other known college and university to join in the commemoration.

Today, the proliferation of campuses and the relative short tenure of presidents makes it unfeasible for any institution to send a representative to every such occasion. It is still correct (although expensive) to send an announcement to all. But most institutions now invite only others with whom they have ties.

When the occasion is a presidential investiture, invitations should be sent to all institutions where the new president has studied. To invite delegates, send an invitation to each president and allow him or her to appoint someone to represent that institution. For convenience and economy, a delegate may be an alumnus who lives in the area.

On procession day, the marshals are responsible for making sure that delegates are lined up properly. Delegates march in the procession according to the year of their institution's founding (oldest first). This can be a prickly situation, because many are quite snobbish about their founding year and take offense if they are not assigned the correct position in line. To avoid confusion, organize the lineup on paper, and coordinate with the marshals so that everyone knows who should be where. Problems will be avoided if all marshals have the lineup and a list of founding years with them. This precaution is enormously helpful when unexpected delegates arrive.

Escorts

Prominent faculty members, preferably from the honored guest's discipline, are assigned to host and escort honorary degree candidates not only in the procession, but throughout their stay in town. The escort meets the candidate at the airport and accompanies him or her to all official functions associated with commencement. It is the escort's duty to introduce the guest and help him or her feel at ease. Escorts transport the person around campus and are responsible for delivering him or her to the ceremony on time.

Greetings

Institutions that choose not to send a delegate may instead send greetings. Traditionally, greetings were sent in Latin because it is the international language of scholars, but today most greetings are in English.

Greetings are conveyed via a document, sometimes beautifully hand-lettered, and extend congratulations and good wishes from one institution to another. Some institutions display greetings during the celebration. Afterward, greetings should be cataloged and stored in the archives.

Hood Marshals

It is almost impossible for a graduate to place a hood over his or her head with any degree of dignity. A solution for this problem is to appoint faculty members or other persons to be hood marshals.

Hood marshals are part of the dais party, and normally, two hood marshals are needed for each graduate. While the president reads the candidate's citation, the marshals slip the hood over the graduate's head. The president then hands the graduate his or her diploma. In many schools, the hood marshal is the candidate's major professor who bears the hood, sits with the candidate, and presents the candidate to the president.

If degree recipients will be seated on both sides of the dais, it is best to have marshals stationed on each side as well, simply to avoid having them go back and forth across the stage as the candidates within each discipline are called in alphabetical order. Always practice hooding so that candidates know what to expect. It is preferable to team inexperienced hooding marshals with those who have experience in accomplishing this sometimes awkward ceremony.

Marshals

The name "chief" (or head or faculty) marshal refers not only to a ceremonial office but to the person who holds that office. The chief marshal's job is to lead the academic procession and act as the institution's chief protocol officer.

Serving as chief marshal is an honor usually reserved for an eminent faculty member. The chief marshal wears special regalia, usually a ceremonial doctor's gown in the colors of the college or university. Otherwise, the person wears his or her own regalia.

Originally, a marshal was a high official in a royal court, and it was his job to arrange the military line of attack. Today's marshals perform a similar function by leading processions and keeping order within an assembly. The chief marshal is assisted by other people, usually young faculty members, who lead divisions (such as colleges) within the procession and also serve as ushers. These people are referred to as junior, associate, or assistant marshals, although occasionally the Old English term "beadle" is used. The college or school marshals carry small batons as symbols of their authority.

One important function of the marshals is to ensure that everyone lines up in the correct order. Members of visiting institutions are lined up according to year of founding, with the oldest marching first. (Have a list of founding years on site, because delegates may not know their institution's date.) Faculty line up according to seniority, with the most junior members going first. Also, it is courteous to appoint marshals to guide VIPs, the spouses of honorary-degree candidates, and members of the dais party to their seats.

During the ceremony, marshals are seated in the first row of the delegation they escorted. Plan to have two marshals stationed per seating section and two to escort each division of the procession. Marshals also supervise student ushers, who are sometimes called by another Old English term, vergers. This name originally referred to the officers who stood at either side of a bishop or king to protect him as he stood at the verge of danger. Student ushers are usually recruited from student service organizations.

The chief marshal might also serve as the mace bearer, but many institutions select an additional person, who becomes part of the marshal's staff, to fill this function. Regardless of who bears it, the mace is closely associated with the marshal's office. The mace represents the civil authority of the institution, and by bringing it into a gathering, the marshal is symbolically displaying that authority to guests. For this reason, the mace opens and closes every formal ceremony of an institution. If your campus does not have a mace, or if the mace is carried by someone else, the marshal's symbol of office is a baton, and he or she should carry it at the head of the procession. The chief marshal and the mace bearer are seated on the dais, where the marshal may also serve as master of ceremonies.

• • •

Order of Processions

Academic processions are based on clerical processions developed over centuries by the Roman Catholic Church and the Church of England. Dignity, pageantry, and pomp are desired elements.

Regardless of this history, the order of march and whether it should begin with the highest- or lowest-ranking guests has been a matter of debate for years. Traditional protocol dictates that the last position is the place of honor, and therefore the dais party, including the president, should enter last. There are many examples to support this. When Her Majesty Queen Elizabeth II enters an assembly, everyone else must already be in place. This is a sign of respect. During the opening ceremonies of the Olympic games, the most honored element, the torch, enters last. At a wedding, the bride enters last. A solid argument for having the platform party enter last can also be made from a practical standpoint: If the dais party enters first, there is a limited audience to enjoy the most symbolic and beautiful elements of the ceremony, the entry of the mace, and the splendor of the president in full regalia. Protocol is based on deference, and deference in an academic procession would indicate that the dais party has earned the right to process after all others have found their seats.

In 1959, a committee of the American Council on Education said that reversing the procession's order, that is, having the platform party enter first, is also acceptable. This decision has led to confusion and a variety of processional arrangements, many of which compromise the traditions that give academic ceremonies much of their meaning and beauty.

Regardless of which order you chose, the most important thing to remember as you form the procession is that dignity is the essence. This is not an appropriate time for self expression through whirlygigs attached to mortarboards or dirty running shoes on the feet of platform participants. Marchers form in ranks of two except when a person is being singled out for special attention—for instance, a president about to be inaugurated would walk alone. Marchers should be encouraged to walk not with military precision but with a natural step at a dignified pace. All members of the procession must wear regalia with the exception of military personnel, who wear their dress uniforms, and members of religious orders, who wear their habits or ceremonial dress.

The orders of march that follow are based on the traditional low-to-high order. They can also be followed in inverse order. Recessionals are always in high-to-low order: The president and dais party exit first.

• • •

Commencement

The graduation ceremony is the capstone of the academic year; after all, graduating students is the reason the institution exists in the first place. In recent years, large graduating classes and rowdy behavior have necessitated some modification of the traditional ceremony to facilitate crowd control, especially with regard to the entry of the seniors. If you have a very large class, one option is to have members enter the arena via multiple side entrances before the procession begins. The order:

Students enter and remain standing
Processional to music:
Head marshal
Color guard
University symbol (college banners or other symbols)
Faculty beginning with instructors, assistants, lecturers, and associates

Professors by rank (in order of seniority, newest first)
Administrative personnel and emeriti
University senate
Deans
Candidates for honorary degrees and their escorts
The platform party (all remain standing until the president sits):
    Trustees
    Master of ceremonies
    Honorary-degree recipients and their escorts
    Speaker (if any)
    Vice presidents
    Provost
    Mace bearer
    President

During the recessional, the audience remains seated, which reverses the order and is led by the mace bearer, followed by the president, then the dais party, then the first row of faculty, and so on until all members of the opening procession have left the hall. If the institution is large, faculties and students do not recess.

A standard order of events for the commencement ceremony is this:
The National Anthem
Music, either vocal or instrumental
Address by the president or guest speaker
Conferring of degrees in course
Alma Mater
Conferring of honorary degrees, awarding of prizes or medals
Music
Farewell
Recessional

An alternative format:
Welcome
The National Anthem
Invocation
President's address
Greetings from the state system's board of regents or trustees
Conferring of honorary degrees
Commencement address by a guest speaker
Conferring of degrees and presentation of diplomas
Alma Mater
Recessional

• • •
Convocations

Convocations are held for a variety of purposes, from awarding honorary degrees to distinguished persons who cannot be on campus at commencement time, to celebrating anniversaries, to opening the new academic year. The order for convocations is identical to that used for commencements except that representatives of student government join the faculty following the campus symbol. Convocations sometimes include unique elements that give local flavor. Examples might be a group of Native Americans in traditional dress at a Southwestern university or a company of pipes and drums at a campus with a Scottish heritage. Otherwise, follow the commencement pattern for both processional and recessional. If you are including people who may not have previously been part of an academic procession, it is a good idea to explain procedures carefully. If the honored guest is a head of state or an official of another country, it is a nice gesture to play the country's national anthem. Do this before "The Star-Spangled Banner."

• • •
Inaugurations

Traditionally, the term "inauguration" means a large celebration that encompasses a series of public events, including a lecture, a theatrical production, and a musical performance given in celebration of the installation of a president. The installation is the actual moment the president is conferred with the articles of office. When the ceremony is smaller and more private, it is called an investiture.

The main reasons for an inauguration are to introduce the new president to your constituents and provide a platform for the new leader to publicly state his or her vision. Like other academic ceremonies, inaugurations are firmly grounded in medieval traditions. There is no single correct inauguration or installation ceremony. The new president's preferences should be ascertained early, before plans begin to develop and become difficult to change. He or she may prefer to be installed during commencement instead of spending time and money to stage a separate inauguration.

An appropriate order of march would be this:
Chief marshal
Color guard
Symbols of the institution (banners)
Student representatives
Alumni representatives
Delegates from learned societies
Delegates from other college and universities
Faculty by rank
Deans and directors of schools and colleges
Your institution's principal officers

Emeriti trustees

Trustees

Mace bearer

Chair of the trustees, governor, or whoever is officially conferring the title on the new president. (When a retiring president is taking part in the ceremony, the mace bearer walks before him or her. The retiring president would be followed by the chair of the trustees or the governor of the state, whoever is performing the installation.)

The dais party:
   Speakers
   Other members of the platform party
   The new president

The recessional is in the reverse order, with the exception that the mace bearer now walks before the new president.

CHAPTER 6

International Relations

*A*S SPECIAL EVENTS PLANNERS, WE orchestrate not only the formal details of visits (ceremonies, speeches, guest lists, and the like) but many of the most personal details of food, housing, and itineraries. The decisions we make affect everything from how visitors view the quantity and quality of our hospitality to how well they feel during their stay.

It is important to recognize that there are many differences between cultures. When guests step off a jet on U.S. soil, they have not left behind their concept of "normal" any more than we would upon arriving in their country. Our bodies are conditioned to eat certain foods at specific times of day, to drink favorite beverages, and to sleep on a routine schedule. (It's the rare traveler who doesn't eventually long for "home cooking.") In each culture, expectations of what constitutes good manners and acceptable behavior have been conditioned since birth. Arriving in a different country instantly changes every one of those norms. While part of the reason for visiting is to catch a glimpse of another way of life, part of our job is to soften the edges and do everything possible to make our guests feel comfortable and well tended.

Americans are noted for a casual lifestyle that includes less formality in entertaining than one might find elsewhere and less adherence to the polite rituals that are considered essential to appropriate behavior in other societies. An example is the American habit of immediately addressing a person by his or her first name. In many cultures, such familiarity is deemed inappropriate. Many cultures observe specific rules for greeting visitors, exchanging gifts, touching, posture at the dinner table and in meetings, and hand gestures. There are wide differences in concepts of personal space, eye contact, and even the meaning of smiles. Before foreign government officials or other international visitors come to call, it is essential to research and observe appropriate etiquette and protocol.

• • •

Protocol for Government Officials

Campuses are favorite stops for religious leaders and heads of state. In 1994, Regis University in Denver simultaneously hosted the president of the United

States and the Pope. Former Soviet President Mikhail Gorbachev was a guest of honor at the 250th-birthday celebration of the University of Virginia in 1993. And Rice University hosted the leaders of what were then called the G7 nations during the Summit of Industrialized Nations in 1990. In each case, matters of protocol demanded careful attention and extra planning.

The term "protocol" refers not to good manners but to a system of rigid rules about international courtesy and the official manners observed when government representatives take part in ceremonies. These rules have evolved over hundreds of years and are strictly followed. Ignorance of them can cause great embarrassment for your institution and discomfort for your guests. Protocol must be observed any time a foreign government official visits your campus.

Much of protocol revolves around precedence, which is the recognition of an individual's rank. Worrying about who outranks whom in the manner of the courts of Europe was a concept Americans threw off with the Revolutionary War. In the world of international diplomacy, however, precedence remains very important, and the tradition is observed in the United States for this reason. Errors on this point alone can cause strained relations and embarrassing situations. Precedence plays an important role in introductions, receiving lines, seating for dinner, and toasting. In her book, *Protocol*, Mary Jane McCaffree says, "Failure to recognize the proper rank and precedence of a guest is equivalent to an insult to his position and the country he represents."

When preparing to host international government officials, call your guests' countries' consulates for advice on everything from who outranks whom to name pronunciations, culture, foods, and traditions. If there is no consulate in your area, call the country's embassy in Washington, DC. Ask to speak to the cultural attaché.

In the United States, the Department of State's Protocol Office is responsible for such matters.

• • •

Welcoming International Visitors

- Research your guests' countries and customs. Learn about history, culture, language, religion, and attitudes toward women. Know major cities and basic geography. Learn about a few famous citizens. Research attitudes toward Americans.
- Research the titles of each member of the party. Understand rank and status and be prepared to use titles correctly. Be prepared to make proper introductions. Don't call people by their first names; in some countries, the use of first names is reserved only for family and very close friends. In Britain, France, and Germany, for example, it is not acceptable to use first names until invited to do so.
- Know the sequence of the name. Not all cultures use first name, middle name, last name as is customary in the United States. In some cultures (China for one) the family name, or what Americans would consider a person's "last name," is given first.

- Prearrange all accommodations and transportation. Provide a car and driver for the duration of your guests' visit.
- Plan a light itinerary for the first day so people can rest from the trip.
- Greet guests at the airport, and escort them from place to place. The manner in which foreign guests are greeted (or not) can set the tone for the entire visit. Many cultures have important welcoming rituals. Research these customs and follow them. For example, the appropriate welcoming for the Dalai Lama is the exchange of white silk scarves at the airport the moment he arrives. A scarf is offered draped over the outstretched arms of the university president, as the highest-ranking official on campus, as he or she bows. In turn, the Dalai Lama presents the president with a white scarf.
- Learn about handshaking customs. Expectations vary widely from the firm American handshake to the limp Japanese grip.
- Research gift-giving customs.
- Provide guests with a written list of the persons they will meet and their titles. Include telephone numbers of persons who can be called in case of questions or problems. Provide this information in their language as well as in English.
- Provide a detailed itinerary of the visit including titles of all persons involved.
- Provide letters of introduction in the foreign language.
- Have your business cards printed in English on one side and in your guest's native language on the other. Be certain both sides look equally nice. Present your card with your guest's native language facing up.
- Retain a competent interpreter. Meet with him or her in advance to discuss the visit and familiarize him or her with any technical terminology that may be used.
- Learn and use a few basic words and greetings in your guest's language.
- Provide agendas, meeting handouts, audiovisuals, and technical documents in your visitor's language. Convert measurements from English to metric.
- Research dietary and drinking customs so that you do not inadvertently serve a food or beverage that is considered taboo. If you are hosting a dinner, provide your guests with a program or agenda printed in their language so that they aren't left wondering what is about to happen.
- Rehearse toasting customs so that your campus representative is prepared to offer and reply to toasts.
- Research customs about the concept of time and punctuality.
- Know what topics should be avoided in conversation. Never criticize the guest's country or its policies or administration.

• • •

Resources for Assistance

On your own campus, call on international-studies faculty who are familiar with other cultures, and enlist the services of foreign-languages faculty to serve as interpreters and hosts. Prepare a briefing paper for your campus representatives on the visitor's culture, rehearse ceremonies (such as bowing), and teach staff how to say common phrases in the visitor's language.

• • •

How to Work with an Interpreter

Whether your institution is sending a delegation abroad or welcoming international visitors itself, chances are that there will be times when an interpreter will be essential. The skills of someone who can accurately communicate not only the literal but the intended meaning of words is particularly important if speeches, presentations, technical explanations, and toasting will be part of the visit. Here are some tips for finding and working effectively with an interpreter as suggested by international expert and author Roger E. Axtell in his book, *Do's and Taboos of Hosting International Visitors.*

Interpreters deal with the spoken word, translators with the written word. Most interpreters are now trained to provide language equivalents, not literal word-for-word translation. This technique helps to preserve the sense or intended meaning of the speaker's words instead of providing a literal translation of each word spoken.

Interpretation can be simultaneous or consecutive. A simultaneous translation means the interpreter is converting one language to another as the person speaks. This technique is the most difficult and most prone to error. In consecutive interpretation, the interpreter listens to the speaker, relays the meaning to the listener while the speaker is silent, then turns back to the speaker to hear the next message.

Hire an interpreter who is familiar with the region and customs of the people you are visiting or hosting. There are many regional dialects, accents, and word meanings within the same language. Interpreters trained in British English (as many foreign interpreters are) may not understand the slang, colloquialisms, or humor of American English. The Spanish that is spoken in Mexico is not the same as the Castilian Spanish used in parts of Spain. The French spoken in Quebec varies slightly from that used in Paris.

Always hire a professional interpreter. Begin by checking with faculty in your foreign-languages department, or, if you live in a city, check the Yellow Pages under "translators." Interpreters are usually paid by the day or hour; translators are generally compensated by the word.

Make a Plan

Meet with the interpreter in advance to discuss the meeting's purpose and agenda and to acquaint him or her with the names, ranks, and titles of your guests. Reviewing technical or unusual terms and giving the interpreter an advance copy of speeches, technical material, and handouts will be greatly appreciated and help ensure accuracy. A face-to-face meeting will also give the interpreter a chance to observe the speaker's pace of speech, learn his or her voice, and become familiar with his or her accent.

If your president or other official will make a speech, it is best to have him or her rehearse with the interpreter. Speeches should consist of short but complete sentences. Prearrange signals so that the interpreter can alert the speaker to speed up or slow down.

During a Meeting

The interpreter is not a guest but should be treated with the same courtesies extended to everyone else. Most interpreters will choose not to eat while they are working, but do provide a meal either before or after the event. Tell the interpreter the dress code for each activity.

During a meeting, seat the interpreter between the two principal parties. He or she should sit back from the table slightly so that the two people communicating can see and hear each other clearly. When high-ranking diplomats, government officials, or heads of organizations are involved, the interpreter should be seated in a small chair between, but slightly behind, the two main representatives. He or she should be unobtrusive and should not eat if a meal is being served.

Look at the person to whom you are speaking, not at the interpreter. Pause between sentences to allow the interpreter time to convert your words. Allow time for the interpreter to explain audiovisuals. Don't use slang or profane language or tell dirty jokes.

It is acceptable to ask the interpreter questions or to discuss fine points to be certain he or she understands your meaning and can thus convey it precisely.

Interpreting for Audiences

Simultaneous interpretation is usually used for speeches to large audiences. The interpreter needs a separate microphone.

Plan for the speech to take twice as long to allow for the interpretation. Provide interpreters with a copy of speeches. If you are hosting an international meeting, provide multilingual signs, agendas, handouts, and name badges. Staff registration and information desks with multilingual personnel.

Flowers Say Many Things

In many cultures, flowers and flower colors have strong meanings. Because special events planners almost invariably use flowers in centerpieces or send them as gifts, it is important to know which flowers are not welcome by your guests. To people from Belgium, France, Germany, and Italy, chrysanthemums (especially white; for Germans, yellow) are associated with death. Giving them or using them in a centerpiece would be the equivalent in our culture of a bouquet of black roses. To the Japanese and Chinese, "death" flowers are white, to Brazilians they are purple, and to Mexicans, purple or yellow. Red roses indicate romantic love in Austria, England, Germany, and Switzerland. Sending them says, "I love you."

• • •

Gifts Are Important

The exchange of gifts with international visitors is more important than most Americans realize. Be prepared to exchange gifts by having a selection on hand of items that are of high quality and small enough to be shipped. Be certain the products are American-made. Good choices are packaged food products from your state, locally made candies, crafts, or a picture book about your state or institutional history. A framed photo of your guests taken on campus is a meaningful memento.

Research gift-giving taboos. For instance, don't give a gift wrapped in white paper to someone from Japan; white means death. Don't give someone from China a clock—it connotes the ticking away of time and is equivalent to saying "I wish you were dead." You will insult a visitor from Egypt by wrapping a gift in green paper, because green is the national color. In many Latin American countries, a gift of knives is superstitious and means the severing of a relationship. Many foreigners will be insulted by a miniature of their country's flag, especially if it is embroidered on apparel. Take it easy on logo items, including institutional logos, as many foreigners will consider these things to be tasteless forms of self-promotion. Never give gifts of liquor or products made from animals that scavenge (like pigs) to Muslims, as these are forbidden by their religion. For the same reason, don't give leather products to people from India; to a Hindu, the cow is sacred.

The presentation of the gift can be as important as the gift itself. Research how and when this is accomplished according to good manners in your guest's country. You will embarrass your Japanese guests and cause them to lose face if you present them with a gift before they have offered you one. In some cultures, it is not appropriate to exchange gifts in a business setting; in others, gifts are not exchanged at a first meeting but later in the visit. Etiquette calls for the Chinese to refuse a gift several times before accepting.

Gifts should be beautifully wrapped, as neglecting to do so is seen as bad manners in many cultures. But check color meanings before selecting a paper. In China, gifts are usually wrapped in red for good luck. White paper means death. To the Japanese, white, black, and red are for funerals. Don't enclose a business card; instead write a personal note on a blank notecard. Don't be surprised if the gift is not opened in your presence, and don't force the issue.

Most gifts are exchanged at the end of the visit, but do your homework to determine whether you will also need gifts upon arrival, only at visit's end, or for both occasions. If you haven't received anything by the end of the visit, downplay the presentation of the gifts you are giving, and offer them as a memento or souvenir of the occasion. If you are presenting only one gift, give it to the highest-ranking member of the party, and emphasize that it is given from your institution to his or her institution or company (not as a personal gift from your president to the individual). If you are giving gifts to everyone, be certain that identical presents are given to all persons of equal rank.

For more information and advice for specific countries, a visit to the international business section of a large bookstore should yield a selection of up-to-date books on how to do business abroad.

• • •

What's for Dinner?

How much food is provided, what is served, and when it is offered are very important considerations. Anyone who has ever traveled knows that it doesn't take long before jet lag, odd schedules, and unfamiliar foods take their toll. You can help minimize the damage by being considerate of the differences in what and when people eat.

In many nations, the main meal is eaten at midday. But midday might be anywhere from 1 to 3:30 p.m., not noon as is the U.S. custom. Dinner, served in the States anywhere from 5:30 to 7 p.m., doesn't begin until after 8 p.m. in many countries. In Spain, dinner is often eaten after 10 p.m.

Eating on the run between meetings or discussing business over a meal is an American phenomenon that will seem improper to many visitors. In contrast to our hurried pace, in many other countries meal times are important opportunities for socializing and building relationships. Instead of burgers in a bag, lunch can take two hours, and it is polite to linger and enjoy conversation. Many people then take a nap or rest period and resume work in late afternoon.

Being considerate of your guests' regular dining patterns can go a long way toward making their visit more pleasant. If you are hosting people who are accustomed to eating a large meal at midday, an American light lunch might leave them feeling hungry and cranky. Ask when they prefer to eat their main meal. Note meal times on itineraries so there is no confusion.

Another American habit—the breakfast business meeting—is something that is simply not done elsewhere. Many visitors will consider the idea positively barbaric.

Research and observe your guest's dietary taboos. Buddhists and Hindus do not eat beef and are most likely vegetarians. Muslims and some Jews are strictly forbidden to eat pork or any other animal that scavenges. This includes some fowl and sometimes lobster or crab. Be mindful of the many products that include pork—lunch meats, hot dogs, ham, sausage, bacon, and pâtés, to mention a few. Muslims do not consume alcohol, including that used in cooking. Many Jews eat only a kosher diet that governs the manner in which food is prepared and prohibits eating milk and meat or poultry together. And one of America's favorite vegetables, corn, is considered by many Europeans to be suitable only for animal feed.

After determining what to serve, consider carefully where to serve it, because the status of the setting is often interpreted as sending a message. It is a high compliment to choose an exclusive setting, like the president's home, an official guest house, or another private home. As a planner, hosting a catered meal in one of these locations as opposed to using a restaurant or club gives you the advantage of greater control of the food and flow of events.

• • •

What's to Drink?

Cocktail hours are an American invention and a custom that many visitors may not enjoy. Most foreigners find our mixed drinks too sweet, and most don't combine alcohol and ice cubes. American beer is weak and overly carbonated compared to European brew, which is typically stronger, darker, and served at room temperature. In Europe, wine is a common accompaniment to dinner.

Generally speaking, when hosting international visitors, dispense with the cocktail hour or shorten it to the time it takes to consume one drink, and serve only wine.

CHAPTER 7

Hosting People with Disabilities

$\mathcal{A}$PPROXIMATELY 35 MILLION PEOPLE IN THE
United States have disabilities. With the aging of the
population, the number of people who have impairments
of mobility, sight, and hearing will certainly grow. Being prepared to accommodate
them graciously is part of polished special events planning. The first rules are to
focus on a person's abilities rather than his or her disabilities and to be certain your
facilities and staff are ready to serve all guests.

First, check access to the venue. Walks, curbs, ramps, entrances, corridors,
elevators, drinking fountains, restrooms, and public telephones should all be
wheelchair accessible. Develop a list of community resource people who provide
sign-language interpretation, wheelchair-accessible ground transportation, and
wheelchair rental and repair before you need their services. Teach events and
waitstaff how to interact with people who have impairments. The suggestions in
this chapter are from two excellent sources. *Business and Social Etiquette with
Disabled People*, by Chalda Maloff and Susan Wood is a comprehensive guide to
hosting disabled guests. Another valuable resource that belongs on every special
events planner's bookshelf is *Accessible Meetings and Conventions*, by Jane E. Morrow,
Ph.D., and Critta B. Park. Published by the Association on Higher Education and
Disability, the book contains the text of the 1990 Americans with Disabilities Act
and is jammed with important technical information about accessibility that events
planners should know.

• • •

You're Invited

Invite people who have disabilities to all functions you believe they might
enjoy whether or not you think they are capable of attending. Issue invitations far
enough in advance so that anyone who wants to attend has ample time to make
arrangements for special transportation or other needs. Include a check-off line on
R.S.V.P. cards for guests to indicate if they need handicapped-parking permits or
other accommodation. This should be done even if you invited essentially the same
group a few weeks earlier and no one required special services; you may be surprised

to learn that one of the trustees has a leg in a cast and requires a wheelchair. It is wise to telephone all guests who mark the box to ensure that you are aware of their specific needs.

• • •

Wheelchairs, Canes, and Crutches

Most people who use a wheelchair, cane, or crutches manage in almost every situation without assistance. Ask before lending aid, and find out specifically what needs to be done before making physical contact with the person. Wait for instructions, and once your offer to help has been accepted, follow through unobtrusively.

For dining, wheelchairs can be accommodated at standard 30-inch-high tables. It is best to seat wheelchair guests in the middle where there are no table legs and to allow extra room between tables and at the table to accommodate the chair. If you are planning seating for tables of 10 guests, remove one place. Thus, the table would accommodate eight guests plus the wheelchair, or nine persons total. (Remember to check whether anyone seated on the dais will need a ramp to get to his or her place.) Persons who use a cane or crutches will appreciate a seat against the wall so their appliance can be leaned there within easy reach.

Ready your campus auditorium to accommodate wheelchairs by removing the end seats of several rows. In this way, persons in wheelchairs can be blended into the crowd instead of always being grouped in the back of the room.

Making Conversation

When conversing with someone in a wheelchair, talk to the individual, not his or her companion. Position yourself so that the person can see your face at a comfortable angle. Don't stand at the person's side or crouch down. Have additional seating available in the room so that guests can be seated to talk with persons in wheelchairs from a position that is comfortable for both.

Doors and Elevators

Open a door as a person in a wheelchair or using walking aids approaches, and hold it until he or she is completely through. If the person is partially through the door and is holding or leaning on the door, don't grab it. Chances are the person is using the door for support, and by pulling it, you could cause him to loose his balance.

Hold elevator doors open when you see an impaired person approaching, and keep holding until you are certain all parts of his or her appliance are inside. Ask which button the person would like to have pushed.

Pushing Wheelchairs

Ask before pushing a wheelchair, and never let go or stop steering without telling the person. Motorized chairs don't normally require pushing and can be easily damaged by doing so. Thick carpets, steep inclines, wet weather, or bumpy streets may render a motor inadequate and make a push necessary. Ask first.

When you do push a wheelchair, go slowly and cautiously and take note of the chair's dimensions to be certain it will fit where you are trying to go. Remember that the foot plates stick out in front. Avoid soft spots, potholes, rough terrain, and thick carpet. To get the chair up and down steps or curbs, first ask if person wants help. To go up, lean the chair back and raise the front wheels up over the step and then push the chair up. To go down, first ask if the person prefers to go backward or forward. Either way, elevate the front wheels so the person's weight is supported by the back of the chair and lower the chair down the step.

To assist someone who walks alone but with difficulty, walk at his or her side and offer your arm (not your elbow) for support and balance. If more help is needed, place you arm around his or her waist. If the person can go up or down stairs, follow behind him or her when going up the stairs; go in front when descending. In this way, you can block his or her fall in the event of a stumble.

• • •

Impairments of Hands and Arms

Mobility impairments can also involve use of the hands or arms. Avoid serving these guests hard-to-handle foods like overstuffed sandwiches, spaghetti, peas, or foods with bones like poultry and ribs. Offer to have the person's plate prepared in the kitchen so that it is more manageable by cutting the meat, removing rinds, and opening and fluffing foods like baked potatoes. People who have difficulty using their hands may be more comfortable using a cup with a handle instead of a glass, eating salad from a bowl instead of a plate, or sipping drinks or soup through a straw. These guests may eat slowly, so remind servers not to remove plates too quickly.

• • •

Visually Impaired People

Vision impairments can range from total blindness to limitations that are not readily apparent to others, like the inability to see in low light. Many people who have vision problems compensate with their other senses.

A blind person may be accompanied by a guide dog, use a cane, or rely on a companion to steer in unfamiliar places. It is a misconception that every blind person can read Braille and has a guide dog. In fact, many blind persons use a combination of aids to navigate, and many never learn to read Braille, relying instead on tape recordings or other people who read to them.

Making Conversation

There is no need to speak louder to a blind person unless he also has a hearing loss. Blind persons use voices to get their bearings, so don't stop talking when a blind person enters the room. When you approach a blind person, address him by name so that he knows you are present and can begin to identify your voice. Always say your name until you know the person well enough that he recognizes your voice. Don't worry about using common expressions like "look at that," "see," or "see you later."

Issuing Invitations

Extend invitations to persons with visual impairments by telephone or send a tape. If this is not possible, mail an invitation. Most people who cannot see have someone come on a regular basis to read their mail aloud. Issue the invitation to allow extra time for this to happen. To increase the chances of attendance, offer to provide round-trip transportation. It will probably be most appreciated.

At the Event

Before your guest arrives, check the area for the kinds of things typically associated with special events that pose no more than a nuisance for a sighted person but could cause a person who cannot see to have an accident. Such hazards include extension cords strung across the floor, serving carts left in the hallway, and bus stands tucked beside pillars.

When your guest arrives, it is considerate to offer relevant information about the surroundings. Describe the general scene, and include details about things that could pose a hazard like candles on the tables, a cluster of stemmed wine glasses at each place, or towering floral arrangements that could be knocked over. Other information that may be appreciated is the location of the restroom, a description of the room layout including the position of tables and seating, and the presence of props or room dividers.

If your guest has a guide dog, don't pet, play with, or feed the dog. It is considerate to have a bowl for water available. The dog is working and is trained to follow instructions from its owner. The dog will wait under the table during meals or near the person during meetings.

During the event, a blind person will probably appreciate a seat in a quieter part of the room, because he will rely on hearing to know what is taking place. At dinnertime, briefly describe what is being served, and mention if inedible garnishes are present. Tell the person when he is seated if food is already on the table. Ask if he wants the food on his plate described. If so, visualize the face of a clock and tell what foods are at which position. For example, "Tonight we're having roast chicken breast. It is located at 7 o'clock on the plate. There are green beans pointing from the 11-o'clock to the 1-o'clock position and mashed sweet potatoes with butter covering from about the 4-to 6-o'clock spot. A dinner roll is on the butter plate to the upper left hand side of your plate. The beverage is iced tea." Ask servers not to overfill glasses.

Introductions

Introduce your guest to others. When you are introduced to a blind person, offer to shake hands by saying, "How do you do; I'd like to shake your hand" or simply "Let me shake your hand."

Meetings

If a meeting is part of your agenda, give the blind person the same printed materials that everyone else receives. She can have someone read it to her later. If you have the capability, it is especially considerate to have important information tape-recorded or printed in Braille.

• • •

Hearing or Speech Impairments

Speech and hearing impairments are very common, though often invisible to observers, and can make communication uncomfortable and frustrating for both parties. The first key to success is to be patient. It is not true that most people who are deaf read lips. In fact, most rely on "speechreading," or the combination of a person's lip movements, facial expressions, body language, and gestures. Others use sign language, and many carry a small pad of paper on which messages can be written. Many hearing-impaired people can understand some speech and rely on some lip reading to assist. You can help by facing the person squarely during conversation so that she can see your face clearly. Speak at a moderate pace that is slightly louder than normal. Don't smoke or chew gum or food during conversation because doing so distorts the shape of the lips and face.

When a hearing-impaired person is accompanied by a signing interpreter, greet the interpreter, but speak and interact with the hearing-impaired person as if the interpreter were not present. Don't engage the interpreter in separate conversation; he or she is obligated to relay everything that is spoken in his or her presence. The interpreter is also obligated to hold all conversations in confidence. The interpreter relays what is said verbatim. It is not necessary to preface your remarks with "Tell her . . ."

At the Event

Seat a hearing-impaired person where there is minimal background noise and in good light so he or she can see others clearly. Find out if the individual prefers to be seated in a particular spot. The person may have a "good ear" and desire to have dinner partners seated on that side in order to hear more clearly.

Introductions

Introduce a hearing-impaired person to a few people at a time, not to a large group. Pronounce each person's name slowly and distinctly, and get the conversation started. Don't tell others of the person's disability; let him or her decide whether or not to do so.

Using the Telephone

Assist a hearing-impaired person in using the telephone by acting as an intermediary between him or her and the party who was called. Write down key points of the conversation.

CHAPTER 8

Business Etiquette Basics

$\mathcal{T}$ODAY'S WORKPLACE ETIQUETTE IS GENDER-neutral, and many of the old rules no longer apply. But as much as things have changed, they have also remained remarkably consistent. The purpose of good manners is to make those around us feel at ease. George Washington, writing a school exercise on manners when he was about 16 years old, said, "Every Action done in Company, ought to be with Some Sign of Respect to those that are Present." Throughout his life, Washington was noted as being courteous, respectful, and "spontaneously polite." The hectic pace and impersonal nature of today's society make the need for polished manners even more critical. Knowing what to do and how to do it is empowering. Good manners set you apart and give confidence to deal with any situation. This chapter is a collection of etiquette tips that will help you write your own place in manners history.

Here are some contemporary business etiquette basics:

- Shake hands with everyone, male and female. Shake using one hand, thumb pointing straight up. Pump up and down twice and release.
- Avoid touching people, including back patting, during hand shaking or conversation.
- Introduce people on the basis of rank, not gender.
- Women and men should always stand for introductions.
- Never use trite or sexist nicknames such as "my better half," "dear," "honey," or "sweetie."
- If no one introduces you, introduce yourself.
- Use your full name when introducing yourself.
- Address all women as "Ms.," not "Mrs." or "Miss."
- Open doors for others, regardless of gender. When someone opens a door for you, regard it as an act of politeness and respond accordingly.
- The host of a business luncheon, regardless of gender, chooses the restaurant and picks up the tab.
- Men and women should stick to conservative business dress, even on casual days. Avoid shorts, jeans, sleeveless shirts, tank tops, and anything that is low-cut.

• • •

Welcoming Guests in Your Office

Have a clean, inviting reception area with sufficient seating.

Alert the receptionist that you are expecting visitors.

Be on time. Don't keep people waiting. If there is a delay, make it as short as possible and offer the visitors refreshments such as coffee or soda. Offer to hang up coats.

Go to the reception area to greet guests and escort them to your office. If you can't go personally, stand up, walk from behind your desk, and shake hands when guests are escorted into your office. Indicate where you would like your visitor to sit. If you are expecting more than one person, have sufficient seating prepared in advance.

Don't accept phone calls during the meeting.

When finished, escort the guest to the elevator or lobby.

• • •

Visiting Another Person's Office

When you arrive for a meeting:

- Be on time.
- Give the receptionist your business card.
- Stand until you are shown where to sit.
- Shake hands with the person you are there to see. Introduce yourself if necessary.
- Don't put personal belongings, papers, or samples on the person's desk.
- Don't read what is on the computer screen or on papers on the desk.
- Don't set beverage glasses or cans on furniture. Use a coaster, place a napkin underneath, or hold the drink.
- Never take food of any kind into another person's office.
- Turn off your cellular phone.
- Stick to the subject.
- Be sensitive to clues that the other person is ready for the meeting to end.
- Shake hands before you leave.
- Say a brief goodbye to the receptionist on your way out.

• • •

How Are Your Meeting Manners?

Much of a meeting's effectiveness boils down to manners (or lack of them). A well-managed meeting increases productivity and runs smoothly, largely because the meeting's chair and participants know their roles. Here are some tips for chairing a meeting and for being a good meeting goer.

When You Are in Charge

The first step toward meeting success is having a clear purpose and knowing what you want to accomplish. Define the meeting's objective, and then determine who needs to attend to accomplish it. Invite only the people necessary to fulfill the task. A smaller group will speed things along, and people appreciate not having their time occupied unnecessarily.

- Schedule the meeting for early in the day, preferably so people can stop on their way to work. This strategy lets you harness participants' creativity while they are fresh and energetic and helps ensure attendance because you catch people before they get bogged down in problems at their own offices.

- Set an agenda and distribute it beforehand either in hard copy or by e-mail. Include background information that will help make the time spent together more productive.

- Select and prepare the meeting room for maximum comfort. A room that is brightly lit and cool will help keep people from becoming drowsy. Check the room arrangement by actually sitting in different locations to be certain everyone can see and hear. Cue slides and videotapes, and test AV equipment, especially computer and conference-calling gear. Know what to do if equipment malfunctions or, if you are in a hotel or conference facility, how to contact the on-call AV specialist. Practice dimming and turning on lights. Thoroughly test sound equipment, including all microphones, and adjust volume levels. Tape electrical cords (especially those around the podium) to the floor for safety.

- It is the chair's responsibility to introduce people to one another and to tell them where to sit.

- If your meeting is formal or will involve unfamiliar people, prepare each person a name plate that can be read by others in the room. Assigning seats also gives you the opportunity to seat people together strategically or to keep adversaries separated tactfully. Remember that the second-most-important person present should be seated on the chair's right.

- Begin on time, and don't interrupt progress by stopping the proceedings to fill in latecomers. Instead, keep the meeting moving, and update those who are tardy after adjournment.

- Don't allow phone calls or interruptions, and politely request that cellular phones be turned off.

- Set the tone and establish control by delivering a crisp welcome and very brief overview. Stick to the agenda, and guide conversation to keep things moving on track. Limit circuitous discussion and disagreements, and don't let the meeting disintegrate into bickering or aimless rambling. Settle differences by taking a vote, or, if an issue cannot be resolved, assign the subject to a subcommittee for further study.

- As chair, see to it that people speak in turn and that everyone has a chance to contribute. Call on quiet people to encourage their participation, and tactfully cut off a windy person's lengthy remarks, especially when they are inappropriate or off-subject.

- Take meeting minutes, and distribute them before the next meeting. Minutes serve as a reminder of who promised to do what by when.
- End on time.

Follow Robert

If you work with faculty senate or student government or are asked to chair an important committee, a knowledge of parliamentary procedure will help you do things correctly and speed your meetings along.

The classic work *Robert's Rules of Order* by H.M. Robert is an indispensable handbook. The book was revised in 1990. Look for it in the business reference section of the bookstore.

If mastering the complete Robert's Rules seems a bit daunting, try *The New Robert's Rules of Order* by Mary A. DeVries. Available in paperback, the book offers a modern, simplified version of the original and includes a handy section on meeting planning.

Manners for Attending Meetings

Here's how to project a polished, professional image when you are attending a meeting:

- Arrive on time, prepared for the topics to be discussed by reviewing any background materials that were distributed in advance. If you are making remarks or a presentation, plan and rehearse what you will say. Have your papers and relevant materials neatly organized in a folio or briefcase so that you don't have to dig for them. It is considerate to give your business card to the meeting secretary so that your name can be accurately recorded in the minutes.
- If you are a guest or a newcomer to the group, introduce yourself to the meeting chair or planner. He or she should indicate where you are to sit. If not, ask before taking a seat. Place your briefcase or purse on the floor beside your chair, never on the meeting table. Introduce yourself to others, and make light conversation with the people seated beside you until the meeting begins—unless, of course, they are studying their papers.
- If you are making a presentation that requires audiovisual equipment, arrive early so you have time to test it. Don't leave your slides in the projector unless you are certain no one else will be using it before you. When it is your turn to speak, take your notes to the podium in an attractive portfolio. Don't place them on the podium in advance because other speakers may need room to spread out their notes. Keeping your notes in your possession also prevents them from accidentally being picked up by another speaker when he or she leaves the lectern. Respect others by confining your formal remarks to the amount of time you have been assigned.
- During the meeting, keep attention focused on the purpose at hand by turning off your cellular phone, and refrain from jotting to-do lists,

doodling, or absentmindedly playing with pens, paper clips, eyeglasses, or your hair.

- If no refreshments are offered, don't ask for them. When beverages are served in cans, pour the contents into a glass before drinking. Keep your place at the meeting table free from litter, and place dirty cups on a side table if one is available.
- Don't interrupt others, and suppress the urge to comment on everything that is said. Organize your thoughts before speaking. If you disagree with something that has been said, do so politely and avoid credibility-damaging outbursts of anger.
- When the meeting ends, thank the chair before you leave.

• • •

Orchestrate a First-Class Board Meeting

Board of trustees meetings are occasions that demand organization, accuracy, and extra attention to detail. Every phase of the meeting and accompanying social activities must be orchestrated with the utmost care. In the nonprofit sector, where directors are not usually compensated, a professionally presented meeting is a subtle way of communicating respect for their time. A successful board meeting begins with careful planning weeks ahead of time.

- Announce board meeting dates and locations as far in advance as possible. If dates are known for the entire year, send an announcement at the beginning of the academic year and reminders about five weeks before each session.
- Plan an agenda for each meeting that allows thorough examination of each topic but makes productive use of members' time.
- About one week ahead of the meeting, each board member should receive a packet containing the agenda, all pertinent reports (especially financial information), and the minutes of the preceding meeting and of committee meetings that have taken place in the interim.
- Include a cover letter highlighting any pressing issues and stating the meeting time and place. Provide an overview of other activities to assist members in planning travel itineraries and selecting appropriate attire. Include a travel-arrangements sheet that can be faxed back to you indicating arrival times and transportation needs.
- Give trustees the name and telephone number of a staff member who will be responsible for accepting calls and relaying messages during the meeting. This will reduce interruptions from cellular phones and beepers. It is especially nice to provide each person with this information printed on a small card that can be given to his or her secretary.
- When new board members are added, plan an orientation before their first meeting to update them on campus life. Include a tour, a briefing on important issues and financial information, and the opportunity to meet

the president. Make a point of introducing new trustees to everyone on the board and to all ranking staff members before the meeting begins. New members' photos and biographies should be in board notebooks and published in the alumni magazine. The first meeting that includes new board members is an excellent time to have a professional photographer take an annual group photo.

Be Ready on Site

Several weeks ahead, inspect the board room to be certain it is in tip-top condition. Check whether the carpet or upholstery needs to be cleaned, paint needs to be touched up, or light bulbs need replacement. Test all permanent equipment to see if it is in working condition. Inspect AV equipment for burned-out bulbs or missing parts (especially remote controls).

Reserve the board room for several days prior to the meeting to accommodate impromtu committee meetings and to ensure that it is clean and fresh for the big day.

Order coffee-break and beverage services that use china, not paper products. Request amenities like real cream presented in an attractive pitcher, loose sugar in a bowl, and fresh lemon slices for tea. Use flatware, not plastic spoons or stir sticks. Breakfast pastries, muffins, and bagels should be attractively arranged on platters or in baskets. Never serve from the bakery box. Coffee and other beverage services should be presented on an attractively draped table with fresh flowers or other centerpiece. Keep the coffee fresh, the urn full, and the break area tidy. Consider having the break area set up outside of the meeting room. This makes service easier and quieter and cuts down on the distraction of people getting up for refreshments while the meeting is in progress.

Work with campus security to ensure that parking places reserved for board members are available and that security knows what parking credentials the directors will have and where they are eligible to park. If someone is ticketed, discreetly retrieve the ticket and settle it with the proper office.

Plan the boardroom seating arrangement, and make name cards for everyone who will be at the table. Using name cards on the table is a gracious way of letting people know where to sit and facilitates the use of names during discussions. If reporters attend board meetings, name cards help them accurately identify speakers. (People who are watching the meeting from the room's perimeter do not need name cards.) Though there is no standard name-card size, cards should be large enough to be read from across the table but not so large that they look ungainly. Use a stiff stock, preferably white, that will stand up on its own when folded. Letter in black for readability.

Place the gavel at the chairperson's seat.

Place a pen, a pencil, and a notepad at each place.

Ready a backup supply of the premeeting materials that were mailed out in case some people forgot to bring their copies. Place additional reports and other documents at each seat in an attractive folder.

While trustees are out of the boardroom for breaks, lunch, or other activities, have litter and dirty cups removed, empty trash cans, vacuum if necessary, and push the chairs to the table so that the room always looks fresh. Never disturb personal items or straighten a member's papers. Assign security to guard the room while the trustees are gone.

After the Meeting

- Issue minutes promptly. Include the dates for the next meeting.
- Follow up on action items and summarize assignments for each trustee.
- Process travel-expense and reimbursement requests.
- Thank those who helped make the meeting a success, especially catering and other vendors, campus security, and office support staff.

• • •

Telephone Etiquette Makes a Good Impression

Telephones are such an integral part of our lives that we often take using them for granted. Estimates are that 80 percent of business is now conducted by telephone. Here's how to brush up on your telephone technique and send a clear message every time:

- Treat every call as important. Remember that every time you place or receive a call at work, you are representing your institution.
- Always begin a call by introducing yourself and identifying your employer: "This is Sue Simpson of Upstate University. May I please speak to Ms. Matthews?" Stating your name up front can quickly route you past call-screeners and spares the person who answered the task of having to ask your name. Never assume the person who answers will recognize your voice. Even if you call the number regularly, always give your name.
- Don't accept another call when you are on the line with someone else. Don't use call waiting. It communicates to the person with whom you are speaking that he or she is not as important as whoever is on the incoming call. Additional calls should be routed to another person or to an answering machine and then returned promptly.
- When your phone rings, answer promptly—on the second ring, if possible. When you answer, identify yourself with your name and department.
- If you answer someone else's phone, give his or her name first, then yours: "Ms. Martin's office, Brenda Barnes speaking." Take down the caller's name, phone number, and the message along with the date and time.
- When answering, never say "Who's calling?" If you ask for the caller's name and then say "Ms. Martin isn't in," it sounds as if the caller is not worth her time. It is far better to say, simply "Ms. Martin isn't in" at the outset, then ask for the caller's name and number so the call can be returned.
- Speak clearly and distinctly, and sound friendly. Your voice may be

distorted by background noise or equipment of poor quality. Slow down and be precise, especially when recording a voice mail message.

- Follow through on calls, and return messages as soon as possible, preferably the same day. If you have promised information, call back right away or assign the task to someone else.
- Turn your cellular phone off during meetings or gatherings such as concerts, theater performances, and lectures. When you use a cellular phone, move to a location that will not disturb others and where your conversation can be more private.
- Don't call when people are leaving for lunch, at day's end, or when you know they are on deadline. For example, don't call the catering department at lunchtime to discuss next month's dinner.
- When you are leaving a message, mention a convenient range of times to return your call: "Please tell Ms. Brown that I will be in my office from 2 until 5 this afternoon."
- End the call professionally. Avoid slang expressions like "have a nice day" or "see you later." Instead, thank the person to whom you are speaking and do your best to close the conversation in a way that will make him or her feel satisfied. After saying goodbye, let the caller hang up first, then quietly replace your receiver.

Using Voice Mail

Telephone voice-mail systems and answering machines are great timesavers, helping you send and receive messages more efficiently. Maximize the benefits with these tips:

For outgoing messages, write a brief script and practice saying it out loud before you record it. Once recorded, play it back and re-record if the words aren't clear or your voice isn't enthusiastic. Record at a quiet time when noisy printers aren't running and people aren't talking in the background.

- Always say your name.
- Speak more slowly than normal, and enunciate clearly.
- Give the appearance of accessibility and friendliness by recording daily messages. Mention times you will be in the office so that callers can reach you easily.
- Use your outgoing message to answer routine questions about events. Giving facts about things like ticket availability and critical last-minute news, such as a venue change, can save both you and the caller time and frustration. Keep your recording succinct.
- Don't make callers wait through a laundry list of options and miscellaneous nonsense before they can either record their messages or find out what they need to know.
- Always tell callers how to reach an operator.
- Call your telephone occasionally to monitor the quality of the recording and the clarity of your voice.

- When leaving a message, don't start with your name. Give the listener time to tune in to your voice by saying less important information first: "Hello. It's 9 a.m., Thursday, May 11. This is Sally Stackhouse from the university. . ."
- Say your name clearly. If you have an unusual name or spelling, spell it slowly for the operator to write down.
- Always give your phone number, even if you're certain the person you are calling already knows it. (The person assigned to return calls may not have it.)
- Speak slowly—remember someone is probably trying to write down what you are saying.
- When giving addresses, pause between street numbers and names, between building names and room numbers, and slowly state unique mailing codes. Spell out unusual names that may be difficult to understand: e.g., "Twain Tippets Gallery, Roudebush Receiving Center."
- Cut down on phone tag by giving the person you're calling sufficient information to take action.
- Conclude by once again stating your name and phone number. This spares the listener from having to review the entire message to double-check your name and number.
- Never record confidential information.

When finished, pause for a second before gently replacing the receiver.

• • •

Professional Accessories for Personal Polish

In a typical day, a special events planner may attend campus committee meetings, have lunch with well-to-do volunteers, supervise a room setup, and meet with the president.

Conveying an organized, polished image is key to success. Here are some must-haves for your office and wardrobe that will help give you a put-together, polished, professional image:

- A good pen. Although collectors spend hundreds of dollars on pens, finding one that looks professional and writes well is not difficult, and it doesn't have to be pricy. Try a roller ball style with black ink, and purchase several refill cartridges.
- A card wallet. These small leather wallets are just the right size for holding the business cards you give and receive and a credit card or two. Some have a zipper pouch for a key and change. Card wallets add polish to the ritual of presenting your business card. Because they are thin enough to be stashed in your briefcase or slipped into your suit pocket without making a bulge, they are perfect substitutes for those times when a purse is a nuisance.
- A leather folio. Make a resolution never again to carry a cardboard-backed legal pad to a meeting. Instead, arrive with papers, notepad, business cards,

and pen neatly tucked into a leather folio. Styles and sizes vary. Some have zippered edges. The most popular sizes are letter, which holds standard-size writing pads, and junior, which accommodates 5-by-8-inch tablets.

- A briefcase. Styles have moved away from the mannish, boxy, suitcase looks with snap locks to softer, more roomy models with compartments for everything from a cellular phone to a notebook computer. Saddle tan is a classic color good for year-round use, but black is equally savvy.

- A tote bag. Just because you have to carry supplies and other essentials to event sites doesn't mean you have to look like a pack animal. If you've been using an old canvas giveaway tote or worse yet, a cardboard box, invest in a good-quality tote bag. Totes come in many sizes made from leather, canvas, or nylon. Some have a canvas body with leather straps and reinforcements. Choose a style that is large enough to carry your gear without being too bulky. Look for strong handles and a double bottom.

- A leather desk set. It's time to get rid of the mismatched, plastic desk accessories that were in your office when you were hired and to replace them with your own, high-quality leather desk set. Desk sets typically include a matching desk pad, pencil cup, business-card holder, and notepaper box. Classic colors are dark green, burgundy, and black.

- Personalized memo pads or correspondence cards. Memo pads are 5 by 7 1/2 inches and have your name printed at the top. Use these for brief thank-yous or reminders to your staff—so much classier than using the advertising pads the printer gave you. Correspondence cards are 6 1/2 by 4 1/2 inches with your name printed on the front panel. These are fantastic for personal notes. (Remember to request matching envelopes.) Order either of these items from a printer. Prices will vary according to quantity, type of printing, and paper stock.

• • •

Thank-You Notes

Nothing is quite as meaningful as a sincere, timely, handwritten thank-you note. Immediately following an event, send notes to everyone who helped make it a success, from the florist to the president. Thank-you notes may be handwritten on your campus's preprinted fold-over note cards with matching envelopes, or use a classic 6 1/2-by-4 1/2-inch correspondence card that has black lettering on white or ecru stock. Don't use cards printed with scenes or pictures of kittens, rabbits, bows, flowers, or the like. Never use cards printed with the words "thank you" or those that have a verse.

Thank-yous should be sent no later than the day after the function. Savvy planners keep a supply of stamped stationery on hand so that thank-yous can be continuously written instead of letting the job pile up until it is a time-consuming chore. Keep a list of those to whom you have sent cards.

Telephoning people to say thanks is nice, but it does not release you from the obligation to write a note. E-mail and voice-mail messages are not proper thank-yous.

Bibliography

American Universities and Colleges, Fifteenth edition. New York: Walter de Gruyter, Inc., 1997.

Axtell, Roger E. *Do's and Taboos of Hosting International Visitors.* New York: John Wiley & Sons, 1990.

Baldrige, Letitia. *New Complete Guide to Executive Manners.* New York: Macmillan Publishing Co., 1993.

Claiborne, Craig. *Elements of Etiquette: A Guide to Table Manners in an Imperfect World.* New York: William Morrow and Co., 1992.

Feinberg, Steven L., ed. *Crane's Blue Book of Stationery.* New York: Doubleday, 1989.

Gunn, Mary Kemper. *A Guide to Academic Protocol.* New York: Columbia University Press, 1969.

Holberg, Andrea, ed. *Forms of Address: A Guide for Business and Social Use.* Houston: Rice University Press, 1994.

Jarrow, Jane, and Park, Ciritta. *Accessible Meetings and Conventions.* Columbus, Ohio: Association on Higher Education and Disability, 1995.

Maloff, Chalda, and Wood, Susan Macduff. *Business and Social Etiquette with Disabled People.* Springfield, Illinois: Charles C. Thomas Publisher, 1988.

McCaffree, Mary Jane and Innis, Pauline. *Protocol: The Complete Handbook of Diplomatic, Official and Social Usage.* Washington, DC: Devon Publishing Co., 1989.

Pachter, Barbara, and Brody, Marjorie. *Complete Business Etiquette Handbook.* Paramus, New Jersey: Prentice-Hall, 1995.

Post, Elizabeth L. *Emily Post's Etiquette.* New York: HarperCollins, 1992.

Sheard, Kevin. *Academic Heraldry in America.* Marquette, Michigan: Northern Michigan College Press, 1962.

Tuckerman, Nancy, and Dunnan, Nancy. *The Amy Vanderbilt Complete Book of Etiquette.* New York: Doubleday, 1995.

Viola, Joy Winkie. *Presidential Inaugurations: Planning for More than Pomp and Circumstance.* Washington, DC: Council for Advancement and Support of Education, 1993.

Visser, Margaret. *The Rituals of Dinner.* New York: Grove Weidenfeld, 1991.

Index

*A*PRIL L. HARRIS is a 1975 journalism/public relations graduate of Bowling Green State University. She also trained at the Protocol School of Washington.

An expert in special events management, she has planned and facilitated the special occasions of academics for more than 20 years.

Through her own company, Harris Communications, she serves as an etiquette consultant and frequently speaks on special events planning. She is also the former publisher of *Events*, an award-winning newsletter for special events planners in higher education.

Her background includes serving as a member of the development and public relations staffs of Bowling Green State University, Baylor College of Medicine, and Utah State University. She is author of several books including the CASE best seller *Special Events: Planning for Success* and *Academic Ceremonies: A Handbook of Traditions and Protocol*.

Harris is executive director of the University of Alabama in Huntsville Alumni Association.